I0428842

The Collective

Cari Lynn Vaughn

© Copyright 2016 Cari Lynn Vaughn
Purple Rose Ink Publications

ISBN-13: 978-1532843655
ISBN-10: 1532843658

Introduction

Growing up, I remember seeing commercials on TV for music Compilations. Usually they were some effort to collect all the top hits of country, rock or pop. Billboard and Entertainment Weekly put out some of the compilations. However, it wasn't until the late 1990s and Early 2000's that these compilations became Best Sellers in the form of the NOW Hits Collection. For the most part these were top sellers and the biggest hits.

While I have gathered songs from them at various times, I've never enjoyed the CDs in their entirety. I tend to like random and obscure bands and songs. I often contemplated marketing my brand of off-brand music, but didn't know where to begin.

I've been making Music Compilations since about 1988, when I was 12. In any case, I first I feverishly recorded things off the radio and onto cassette tape throughout the late 80s. Then I moved onto recording tape to tape and CD to tape.

Eventually, I got all my music ripped to my computer and burned CDs around 2004. I still don't have an iPod or MP3 player, but I do have a rather vast musical library. My tastes in music are quite varied. Each title in my compilation can usually be prefaced by saying "I" or "I am" hence the idea of The Collective I.

Whitney Houston

It was at my birthday party that I was first introduced to Whitney Houston. The year was 1986, I believe. I had invited several friends from school to my party that June and Misty Hall showed up with her debut album in hand as a gift for me.

I didn't own any tapes at age nine. I did, however, own a few 45 records that had been passed down to me by my aunt. Those records were all from 1980 or so and so my music collection was hopelessly limited and outdated. It was nice to get something so new and cool.

Misty was into the latest and greatest music of the time. I remember going down to her house on Whitney Avenue in Shelby and doing gymnastics in the yard as we listened to Michael Jackson's *Thriller*. I was never a huge fan of Michael Jackson, but I did enjoy hanging out with Misty and cartwheeling through her front yard.

Anyway, after my party was over I listened to Whitney Houston and I took to her immediately. I loved to sing her songs and pretend I was a famous singer like her.

Later, I was thrilled to see my new favorite singer on a favorite show of mine—***Silver Spoons***. Poindexter met Whitney on the show and she sang *"Saving All My Love"* to him. As an awkward preteen hearing her sing that they were going to make love the whole night through made me embarrassed. Yet, I still longed to have such a magical romantic moment, one worthy of singing such a beautiful song about.

For some reason *"You Give Good Love"* reminded me Indiana Jones. There is a line "Take this heart of mine" which somehow got connected to **The Temple of Doom.** I guess I both romanticized Indiana Jones as a good lover and connected the gruesome scenes of hearts being ripped out of chests with the line *"Take this heart of mine."* Weird, the way things become associated in our minds.

We got cable in the mid-80s and so I was able to watch MTV. Whitney's *"How Will I Know?"* video was on heavy rotation. Her video for *"The Greatest Love of All"* played a lot too.

In 1987 Whitney's second album came out and I have my Mom get it for me. I enjoyed watching the videos for *"I Wanna Dance (With Somebody That Loves Me)"* and *"Where Do Broken Hearts Go?"* as well as *"Didn't We Almost Have It All."*

For some reason I connected *"Didn't We Almost Have It All"* to Stevie and. I am not sure why. It is a beautiful and sad song in the same vein as her later hit *"I Will Always Love You."* I suppose I felt like I'd had something lost it, though I never really had it to begin with. I really loved the line *"One moment and The Soul Can Last Forever,"* To me it meant that the love I felt had touched my soul and comforted me even if the love was never reciprocated.

One of her little known songs was called *"Miracle."* It was about being pro-life and being thankful the miracle of life. And although I still believe it is a woman's right to choose, I also believe that each life is a miracle to be cherished. I thought the song was moving in any case.

In 1990 she released a song called *"All The Man I Need."* I loved it then, but it really took on a whole new meaning in 1995 when I got with Jason. Every time I heard the song from then on out, I thought of him and the tender relationship that we had. At the time, I truly felt blessed to have found someone to love so deeply.

I went back to the song *"Saving All My Love"* in 1994. It was the song that I played for Paul the first time we were together. Though the song was about having an affair with a married man, I still felt it was appropriate. The song was about forbidden love and the love between he and I was forbidden. He was much older and I was still under age. Though he was divorced, I still felt like he wasn't mine to have.

And when that relationship failed I often played Whitney's song *"All At Once"* from her first album and cried. Although I found the song incredibly melancholy before, it took on a new meaning after that particular heartbreak.

Then *The Bodyguard* came out in 1993. I saw the movie in the theater and got the soundtrack soon after. Although *"I Will Always Love You"* isn't a song I attached to a particular person, I do have fond memories of slow dancing to the song. It never fails to move me whenever I hear it.

It was during the time that I was hospitalized in March that I particularly moved by the songs *"Run To You"* and *"I Have Nothing."* These two songs embodied the need I felt for love and comfort. I longed for another person who could not be mine and I wondered why it was so wrong to long for him. I wondered how people could write songs like those and then turn around and say that needing someone was wrong. If it was wrong why did others express the same feeling that I felt? It didn't feel wrong.

When I started writing poetry, Whitney Houston's songs were often inspiration, as were Madonna's and Mariah Carey's songs. I often used lines from their songs in my own work as a tribute and a jumping off point. But honestly, I was never really moved by anything Whitney Houston produced after *The Bodyguard* Soundtrack.

I know that young performers like Mariah Carey and Christina Aguilera named Whitney Houston as a huge influence. She remained one of the most imitated singers even after her career took a dive.

Mariah Carey and Whitney Houston were often rumored to be dueling divas, but their quarrel was purely speculation. They eventually did a duet together for the movie *The Prince of Egypt.* It was a good song, but it didn't have the emotional impact that either of them had produced for other songs.

I felt bad hearing about Whitney's ups and downs. She never really seemed to get back what she lost even though she kept putting out albums. Hearing about her death saddened me of course. Though she didn't write her own songs, she sang them with great gusto and emotion. She could make you dance and make you cry with her dramatic voice. I know her songs made me feel a great deal and for that I am grateful. She will be missed.

Mariah Carey

Mariah Carey must have her turn. I followed up the two Madonna biographies with the only Mariah Carey biography that I could find. It was just a bit out of date since it was from 2001, but it was still interesting. Of course, I found it lacking. After imagining a whole fantasy world with her, what could possibly ever dive deep enough though?

For some reason I really connected with Mariah on a spiritual level. When I wrote my Mariah Trilogy, I guess I was writing about myself more than anything. I used the lyrics and the images from her videos to create my own story. Truly it feels like a collaborative effort and a joining of her vision with my own.

How did it come to be? In 1990 Mariah Carey appeared on the pop scene. Her success story and vocal gymnastics impressed me right away. I got her tape soon after it came out and listened to it over and over.

The video for *"Vision of Love"* had her on a rather bare set. She was in this huge tree swing and then she wandered around a room with a suit of armor and a large curving staircase. Though a minimal set to say the least, I quickly place her in some sort of medieval fantasy.

I'd already written a story set in my mythical country of *Rushmal Shaylin*. *Destiny Foretold* was a foray into that particular fantasy world. It was a thinly disguised adventure with Mark-Paul, Me and a

Princely narrator. The story explored the familiar theme of free will versus destiny. It was easy to add Mariah into the mix.

The idea behind *Rushmal Shaylin* was that it was a colony of advanced people in the South Pacific—perhaps refugees from Lemuria who lived as if in the Middle Ages during the time of the Roman Empire. Well, the fall of the Roman Empire at least. They were in many ways fish out of water. Mariah herself was an outsider and I could relate. It was a natural step to make her an independent lady who preferred life away from the court.

"I Don't Want To Cry" took place in a country cabin. The imagery from the video—which nearly wasn't—sparked my imagination. To think the first video that was scrapped was her wandering around a studio instead of an old house! My story might never have been if Mariah hadn't demanded a re-shoot!

"Love Takes Time" became my MP anthem and my connection to him. I felt like a part of me was missing and that love would eventually lead me to feel whole again. I love the ocean and the video being shot on the beach made it resonate much more. I always imagined walking down a beach with Mark-Paul and telling him the story of us—of my dream and my feelings for him.

"There's Got To Be A Way" played into my growing political awareness. It felt like 1990 was a year of social activity and concern for the "global village." I added her song to my Peace Compilation along with *"Our House"* by Traci Spencer, *"Tell Me Why"* by Expose and *"Love and Understanding"* by Cher.

"Someday" didn't fit into my world, but it was Paul's theme song. He told me he'd sing the lyrics and think of his ex-wife right after their divorce.

I was so excited when the album *Emotions* came out the fall of 1991. I listened to the tape over and over until I wore it out and had to get another one. Her 2nd album was more R&B and more herself, but still parameters of what the record company thought would be successful. The song *"Emotions"* was pleasant enough, but it was the unreleased songs that spoke to me the most. While *"Can't Let Go"* reminded me of Ohio Brown, it was *"And You Don't Remember"* that expressed exactly how I felt at the time. The melancholy in *"Till The End of Time"* just made my heart ache. And *"So Blessed"* basically became my gateway to experiencing spiritual love. The song had such a profound sense of sacredness about it. *"The Wind"* was so sat that I imagined a great sense of loss for Mariah—much more than just for a friend. It could only be the sort of loss that one experiences for the loss of a child I decided.

So, in the first story Mariah lets go of an old boyfriend, loses a brother and meets the man she will eventually marry. In the 2ns story, she goes on her honeymoon to the home land of her love Terry. The Germanic Tribes and how they became the current countries and cultures of Europe have always fascinated me. I made Terry from that world and Mariah sails with him to be at his home. Inevitably, they are separated when she is kidnapped. She is pregnant with his child and very much alone in the world. Mariah, my character, escapes captivity and gives birth. Terry searches everywhere for her and

10

finally finds her. They sail back to Mariah's home, when the baby falls ill and dies.

In looking back, I am not sure where I got all that from. Perhaps it was an intense sense of loss and sorrow that manifested into the particular emotional journey for me. Maybe that sense of sorrow is what connects me to Mariah ultimately. That utter vulnerability, strength and appreciate of beauty is something we share.

In 1993, Paul was all excited because he'd just purchased Mariah Carey's new album *Music Box*. I took the wind out of his sails a bit by telling him I already had the tape. The summer of 1993 was marked by her song *"Dreamlover."* However, it was the b-side to that single that captured my emotions. *"Do You Think Of Me"* was surely written about her forbidden feelings for Tommy while he was still married. It perfectly echoed my forbidden love for Ben though. That essence of longing once again resonated with me.

"Hero" was uplifting and the line "It's a long road" became my anthem. I had suffered a great deal and wondered if I'd ever find happiness. I was doing my best to stay positive, but it wasn't easy to keep a hold of my dreams.

"Without You" broke my heart and inspired part 3 of the Mariah Trilogy. Much of Music Box was dedicated to memories and day dreams from the past. It wasn't a large leap to make my character become depressed, restless and distant. That was the subtext to her album after all. *"All I've Ever Wanted"* was such a huge romantic song. To have Mariah lose her love and sing that to him when they were reunited fit so perfectly into my story.

"Anytime You Need A Friend" merely stands out as a style change. Mariah straightened her naturally curly hair and got bangs. I cut my hair to look like hers. My hair had been all one length and I was tired of it—even though it took forever to grow out in the first place.

Her Christmas album provided another link to MP. *"Fall On Your Knees"* recaptured the sacredness of *"So Blessed."* I listened to that song over and over—trying to reach that inner sense of divinity.

"Fantasy" became all about Jamie Adkins. It was his fantasy to sleep with sexy Mariah Carey. I kept telling him that she was married and untouchably famous, but he didn't care. I was secretly flattered thinking that perhaps that Jamie was drawn to something Mariah and I shared—that it wasn't just her looks that he lusted after.

Daydream spoke to me about my new relationship with Jason in late 1995 and early 1996. The unreleased songs *"I Am Free"* and *"When I Saw You"* in particular touched me deeply. "Forever" was fun and sweet. *"One Sweet Day"* was a great song, but not favorite.

In 1997 Mariah Carey spread her wings and put out her album Butterfly. My cousin Alecia who has always been more into rap than me thought it was her best album yet. *"Honey"* was fun. *"Butterfly"* and *"My All"* were quite moving. And for some reason, *"Whenever You Call"* always made me think of Ethan McMillan Now, *"Breakdown"* and *"Butterfly"* remind me of what is going on with Jason!

I'd stopped my fantasy story series with her 4th album. Her lyrics were no longer timeless and I could no longer relate to them in the way I once did. However, I did incorporate her divorce into my short general fiction piece, *Spread Your Wings.* Typing up that novella is what led me to read Madonna and Mariah Carey's biographies and it is what led to these musings on their effect on my life.

Anyway, I was eager to get the *Rainbow* CD when it came out, but I was quickly disappointed. It was mostly top 40 and rap songs that no longer felt like my kind of music. I missed the presence of Walter Afanasieff in her writing process. She'd ended her writing partnership with him in an effort to completely break away from Tommy and Sony. The subtext of *Rainbow* was that she was stressed out and unsure of her new relationship with Derek Jeter. The depth of emotion from her earlier work was gone.

Glitter felt even shallower than *Rainbow* and flopped for the most part. The movie had potential, but didn't quite pull it together in the end. It felt like it was missing the soul of her earlier work.

Mariah had thrown herself into her work in order to deal with the pain of her divorce and her work suffered for it. She pushed herself to be productive even when she lacked any real inspiration or artistic vision.

Charmbracelet was a bit better in 2002. I remember one of my students at GTCC had purchased the CD and absolutely loved it. I listened to it from the library and never bought it myself. *"Through The Rain"* and *"Flowers For Alfred Roy"* weren't bad. Her cover of *"Bringing On The Heartbreak"* was perhaps my favorite.

13

Then she lost me again when she put out her twin CDs *Mimi* and *E=Mc2*. Mariah seemed to me too lost in the glitz and glamour of being a pop star. The singles were starting to sound all the same and the lyrics lacked any real heart. *Memoirs of an Imperfect Angel* failed to move me at all. It felt like a knock off of a lot of other artists out there.

Mariah recently got remarried to a younger man named Nick Cannon and they had twins together this May. I have hopes that her new album will be better and that it will be a return to her roots and herself musically. I miss her!

Mad About Belinda Carlisle

Belinda Carlisle became a favorite singer of mine with her song *Heaven Is A Place on Earth* back in 1987. I made sure to put that song on my cassette tape compilation. I'd recently gotten more into music and had started recording songs off the radio. Later, her song *Circle in the Sand* made it onto another compilation as well.

It was her second album that caught my attention, but I'd heard her first solo song *Mad About You* on the radio before. *Mad About You* was even featured on one of my favorite shows during the 80s— *Growing Pains*.

Then her third album *Runaway Horses* came out. I wanted to buy it, but I couldn't afford to. I did get the single *Summer Rain* though. One of my favorite things to do was put on what I called my "peasant dress" and go out in the rain and dance to the song. My mother worried that the dress was see-through, but I didn't care. It was dark and no one was looking at me in my backyard anyway.

Eventually, I made up a routine to *Summer Rain,* imaging an invisible partner that I danced with. Who was my partner? Mark-Paul Gosselaar of course! One magical night I could have sworn I saw him materialize before my eyes and fade away. When I went back and rewrote my story *Damon's House* about my past life with Mark-Paul Gosselaar, I included the song in the story.

Around the same time I came up with a special dance to Belinda's song *Circle in the Sand*. I was bored one night and listening to music, when I decided to spin around in a circle to the song. Only I didn't just spin, I pivoted on one foot while focusing on the light fixture in the middle of the room. This allowed me to stay balanced and not get dizzy. Little did I know that this dance was exactly like the dance of the mystical Whirling Dervishes!

Though her 1991 album *Live Your Life Be Free* wasn't a huge success, I still enjoyed it. My friends and I loved the song *Emotional Highway*. In fact, we did head-rushes to the song. *Little Black Book* and *Live Your Life* weren't bad either.

Later, I went back and made up a dance to her song *La Luna* from her *Runaway Horses* Album. It reminded me of Ethan McMillan and the story I wrote *Wings of Desire*. which appeared in my first collection of short stories, *Radiant Darkness*. I suppose it reminded me of my characters because they went to Paris and the lyrics of *La Luna* are all about two people falling in love in Paris.

I missed her 1993 album *Real* and her 1996 album *A Woman and a Man*. Neither of those albums sold very well in the USA. She put out a couple of compilations of her greatest hits. I got one of the collections from the library.

In 2010 Belinda put out a memoir called *Lips Unsealed*, which I picked up at the library out of curiosity. Though I found her self-loathing and drug use interesting to read about, I never did understand why I felt a connection to her music. Her music had an underlying sense of spirituality about it, but her life seemed to missing the spirituality hinted at in her songs.

Recently I read that she put out a French album *Viola*. I have not heard it, but I plan to get a hold of it and listen to it.

A Band with Heart

Heart had been around a long time—some 18 years—before I really took notice of them. Their song *All I Wanna Do Is Make Love To You* was a huge hit in 1990 and it made its way onto my compilation that year. Once I knew who they were, I began to hear their songs everywhere on the radio.

What About Love, Never, These Dreams, Nothing At All, Who Will You Run To, There's The Girl and *Alone* played frequently and quickly became favorites.

I also noticed a poster for Heart's **Brigade** album on the all of Zack Morris's bedroom in a few episodes of *Saved By The Bell*. I often wondered if the poster was put there by the prop department or if it belonged to Mark-Paul Gosselaar himself.

All I Wanna Do sparked a conversation with a friend about what we would do in the same situation as the song described. If our husband or boyfriend couldn't give a baby would we have a one night stand to get that baby? I thought I might do it and my friend said she didn't think she would.

Although the song *Alone* came out in 1987 off the *Bad Animals* album, it took on a particular significance to me in 1992. I had feelings for someone and I wanted a chance to get him alone long enough tot talk about those feelings. The *melancholy* sound fit my fear and longing at that time, so it became our theme. Well, my theme since nothing ever actually happened with him.

Though their 1993 album *Desire Walks On* was not a huge hit, but I loved their cover of Donna Summer's *Woman In Me.* The song stirred desire in me and reminded me of the relationship I was in at the time, particularly the lyrics, *"I might be trembling, but I'm not scared. It's just my desire breaking free,"* and, *"Like the dark side of the full moon, I've never showed what I am showing you."*

My friend Nikki loved Heart's song *Will You There In The Morning.* The lyrics *"Now baby you're my obsession, my addiction, my drug. Don't want to be without you when I wake up, oh no!"* really spoke to her and her relationship at the time.

It wasn't until 1994 that I discovered Hearts older songs. My boyfriend at the time had their record *Dog and Butterfly* as well as *Magazine.* I was thrilled to hear their cover of the Harry Nilsson song *Without You.* Mariah Carey had just covered it and it was interesting to hear the differences in each version.

In 1999 the movie ***The Virgin Suicides*** featured two Heart Songs, *Crazy on You* and *Magic Man.* The Heart Song *Barracuda* was included in the *Shrek The Third* movie, but it was covered by Fergie.

After Heart's 1993 album, they went their separate ways for a while. Nancy stayed home in order to focus on raising her family, while her sister toured and made music on her own. They returned to their partnership in 2002. They have produced 3 more studio albums and have been inducted into the Rock and Roll Hall of Fame. None of their new material has moved me or meant as much as their stuff from the late 80s and early 90s, but they still remain a favorite band of mine.

19

When their autobiography *Kicking and Dreaming* came out in 2012, I eagerly got snatched it up from the library to read. There was a lot I didn't know about the rocker sisters, but quickly discovered as I devoured the book in a day. I recommend the book to any Heart Fan!

Garbage Is Not Pure Rubbish

"I'm only happy when it rains, I feel good when things are going wrong, I only listen to the sad, sad songs, I'm only happy when it rains," sings Shirley Manson of the band Garbage. When I heard the song on the radio I knew it could easily be my theme song. She goes on to say, *"I'm only happy when it rains, you want to hear about my new obsession, I'm riding high upon a deep depression."*

The song was not quite like anything I'd heard at the time. It was an infusion of Rock, Alternative, Pop, Electronic and Dance. The lyrics were dark, yet it wasn't accompanied by the usual screaming and cacophony of sounds that often came with such dark lyrics. I appreciated Metal, Punk and Grunge for their rebellious attitudes and their ability to embrace the darkness, but often times the music was too angry and aggressive. I liked the upbeat sound of Pop music, but I found the lyrics lacking and the message often empty. But in Garbage I found exactly the right mix of evanescent sound, dark lyrics and surprising intelligence.

Garbage was formed in 1994 by Duke Erickson, Steve Marker and Butch Vig. Vig had been in various bands throughout the 1980s and had gone on to produce some huge names, including Nirvana, before striking gold with Garbage. The guys decided they wanted a female lead singer and picked Shirley Manson out from her Angelfish video for *"Suffocate Me"* on MTV. She was just the right combination of sass, sarcasm and sexy that would make the band come alive. Never mind that she lived in Scotland and they were living in Wisconsin at that time. They could make it work!

Vig took his talent for remixes into the studio for Garbage's first album. Instead of composing straightforward tracks with traditional instruments, they tore the tracks apart and added in layers and loops. They manufactured backup vocals and included all kinds of electronic sounds. This use of technology in composing gave them their unique sound and their band name. In an interview they said that a friend came to visit them while they were recording their album and told them the mashed-up music sounded like garbage. And so the name stuck, but their success has been anything but garbage.

"Vow" was the first single off their debut album. According to Vig, the inspiration for the song was a newspaper article about a woman who had gone back to get revenge on an abusive husband, "so we thought it would be cool to get a bit of retribution in there." Vig also said he noted violence could also come from psychological stand point by seeing the story of a sado-masochistic couple who could not keep away from each other. Lyrically, Manson claimed "*'Vow'* is about having feelings [of vengeance]. You have to face your feelings of revenge and work out why you feel that way. It's about that conundrum when you're really angry but in reality you're in a pitiful state. Angry, twisted, but deep down, vulnerable. "During promotion for the song, Garbage joked to journalists that "*Vow*" was about John and Lorena Bobbitt.

"Only Happy When It Rains" was the second single. Lyrically, Manson described *"Only Happy When It Rains"* as "about wanting

love but knowing life will always get in the way.... yet not being obliterated by that. It's a song for people that know what it is like to live on the dark side of life. It's about devotion but a different kind. Devotion to the truth and to freedom... and to hell with the consequences." Although Garbage has had many memorable hits, they will perhaps always be known by this song, as it embodies what they are all about.

"Queer" was their third single. Garbage incorporated a sample of the drumline from New Zealand band Single Gun Theory's track *"Man of Straw"* on *"Queer"*; this loop was layered with an additional drum part performed by Madison percussionist Clyde Stubblefield, who was known for being the most sampled drummer in history for his unaccredited part on James Brown's "Funky Drummer" Manson later explained, "It's not, as you might think, to do with being gay, but tolerance…that is that you think you are normal and the rest of the world is freaky, but we're all equally to blame." Garbage did not write the song to particularly appeal to the gay community, however Erikson stated: "The song isn't about sex at all; it's about the loss of innocence."

They also released *"Supervixen"* and *"Stupid Girl,"* which became hits as well. Both songs were about women's roles in relationships and society. Manson stated that *"Supervixen"* "is all about saying 'idolize me, I'm going to give you everything you want, but you have to do something in return'. It's a bargaining song about a relationship." Manson aimed the song *"Stupid Girl"* as a rebuke towards a friend's foolish behavior: "A lot of females still find it difficult to find their own voice in society. It's just that women have a different set of problems from men... make the most of your potential."

Some of my favorite songs, however, were not released as singles. "*Dog New Tricks*" takes on the idea that humans are the ones who have a hard time learning new things. Manson sings, "*Dog new tricks. Nothing you learn will stick, you make me feel so worthless.*" She is getting tired of being with people who don't make her feel special. Perhaps she is even tired of being abandoned time and time again. She continues on to sing, "*Everyone I know has gone, died, left or just forgot to stay.*" Having abandonment issues myself; this particular line resonated with me.

"*As Heaven is wide*" was another unreleased song that I liked. Though not really a Christian song, it used a lot of Christian symbolism in the lyrics. Words like God, Heaven, Angels, Holy and Hell reinforce the theme something sacred being violated. Manson sings, "*My trust was blind you broke the pact. If god's my witness god must be blind. If flesh could crawl. My skin would fall. From off my bones and run away from here. As far from god, as heaven is wide.*" It is a very angry song, and yet she sings it coolly and calmly. You can hear the pain in her voice, but it is not over done.

The last single from the first album was "*Milk*." Manson was inspired by a line in Michael Ondaatje's *The Collected Works of Billy the Kid* ("her throat is a kitchen") and eluded to it in her lyrics for the song. At its base, Manson believed the song was "a seduction, almost like a siren song" The most electronic based song on the album, "*Milk*" is also one of singer Shirley Manson's favorite tracks from it.

24

She told Melody Maker "It's a dichotomy, a paradox. The thing I really like about "*Milk*" is the fact that it's been dismissed by people as the ballad at the end of the album. To me "*Milk*" is the darkest, most hopeless of the songs. People say 'Oh, it's lovey-dovey, so therefore it's a love song'. But it's a very bleak song, it's about loss and the fear of loss; about things you can't have and things you will forever wait for."

Garbage is anything but. They've proven their worth with a solid first album and then several more afterward. I, for one, am always eager to hear anything new they might put out even if nothing will ever recapture the magic I felt listening to the first album. Garbage captured the mood of the moment in society and in my life. And for that, I will always come to associate them with my ever-blossoming self as I expanded my horizons back in 1995 and 1996.

Evanescence

I heard *Bring Me to Life* in the commercial for *Daredevil* back in 2003. I absolutely loved the song and went out and bought the CD shortly after that. I put in the CD and listened to the whole album. I had found a new favorite band.

Bring Me to Life reminded me my relationship with Jason. I had felt dead inside and was in a dark place before he and I got together. In many ways, he brought me back to life. Though it is a bit anachronistic, I think it really fits what happened back in 1995. The song itself is dramatic and beautiful and sad all at once.

My Immortal came to remind me of Ben. He was my first love and even though he was out of my life, I still felt his presence. I wrote the lyrics in my diary to show how the echoed how I felt the summer of 2005. The song is melancholy with a hint of Gothic in it, which captured my mood precisely.

Amy Lee did a duet with *Seether* in 2004 called *Broken*, which I loved. It became the title song for my compilation for 2005. I felt broken inside and this song was a perfect theme for the struggles I was going through that year.

In 2006 Evanescence put out a new album *Open Door*. The First single *Call Me When You Are Sober* struck a chord in me as well. It reminded me of my ex-boyfriend Paul, who was an alcoholic. I mentioned the song in my fictional autobiographic story *Unzipped.* The other singles off the album were good, but I wasn't particularly moved by them. *Lithium, Sweet Sacrifice* and *Good Enough* were all just good enough.

Her song *Lachrymosa* caught my attention as well. This song reminded me of Lake Lachrymose in The *Wide Window* in Lemony Snicket's *A Series of Unfortunate Events.* In 2006, I was also reading the Meredith Gentry series by Laurel K Hamilton. All of these elements combined in my imagination when I wrote my story **Lachrymosa** and I cast Amy Lee as my Esme. My lover was my beloved Mage in the story. He also is a fan of Evanescence.

When Evanescence's self-titled album came out, I got it out of the library right away. It was a good album, but no one song really stood out for me. They released *What You Want, My Heart is Broken* and *Lost in Paradise* off of 2011 CD. They were all good, but I didn't connect with them like I did with their earlier work.

I read Evanescence is coming out with a new CD sometime this year. I look forward to hearing it and hoping to find some inspiration in it!

Rapture

Last night Jason and I decided to go to a club here in Greensboro. I had rested all day and had enough energy to go and I'm glad we did. We went to a club called Enigma, but all they were playing was Hip-Hop and Rap. We asked for our money back and left to find the N Club. The N Club is downtown and is a very cool place to be. They were playing better music—actual music. Imagine that!

The club was in what looked to be an old theater and had a pretty big dance floor. Jason stood and watched as I joined the crowd of dancers. Almost immediately two guys hit on me. The one told me I looked good and to keep dancing. The other just started dancing with me, but I moved away from him after a moment or two. Jason saw and just smiled at me. The club was filled with mostly college kids and some people are age (late 20s). There were some good-looking guys and women there. Some of them were dancing quite well. It was hard to tell at times if the women on the dance floor were friends or lovers as the bumped and grinded close to each other…

Then the song "Rapture" by Iio came on. The words go:
The night I laid eyes on you
I felt everything around me move
Got nervous when you looked my way
And your love moved right in
All this time, my love, where have you been?

MI Amore.

Don't you know

My love, I want you so

Sugar

You make my soul complete

Rapture tastes so sweet

I'm mesmerized in every way

You keep me in a state of daze

Your kisses make my skin feel weak

Always suffering in your heart

Lift our souls like a bird in the wind

Oh, I glide like I'm flying through heaven

I told Jason that as I danced I like I fell in a trance, like my body was moving on its own and I was in my own little world. I was feeling ecstasy and rapture as I saw the lights flash and heard the beat through my body. Dancing with others is seen as sort of clothed sexual experience, but dancing alone can be pleasurable as well...

Later, they played Salt N Peppa's "*Push It*." I began to let myself go wild and push it every time they said to. Perhaps I pushed it a little too much or a little too good—or maybe I was pushing it in my "*I look easy, but I'm not*" outfit. (A short black skirt and black spaghetti strapped top.) Whatever it was, it caused two guys to dance their way over to me. One even began to bump and grind against me. Suddenly I felt his hips brush my rear end and his hands circled my waist. More amused than offended, I gently pulled his hands away and moved off the dance floor. It was time for a break anyway. I was tired and hot. As the floor and the rest of the club became so crowded there was no room to move, I stayed close to Jason and just in my spot in front of him. We were standing right near a bouncer, whom Jason claims was also checking me out. As I continued to move, I thought about the past and how things have changed so much. I've really grown comfortable in my own skin at long last!

Concerts

December 2, 1994 Aerosmith

I left school and came home. I got ready and threw some things in a bag. I went to Alice and Amber's apartment and waited for them to get ready. Around 3pm or so we left, stopping at McDonalds. We took 96 out of Shelby to Ashland. We stopped and got batteries and then hit 71 North to Cleveland. When we got to Cleveland I got off on the wrong exit. I went around in a circle several times before stopping at a BP station for directions. Finally we found the Gund Arena. Then we looked for a place nearby to stay the night. We didn't see any cheap motels, just the Sheraton. Nikki suggested that we check it out. It was $99 a night, but we figured between the three of us we could afford it. After parking the car in the garage for an additional $6 we went to our room on the 9th floor. The view was great!

When we got to the huge packed Arena, we bought T-Shirts and put them on. Ali bought a beer—since she was the only one of us that was 21 years old. We found our seats in the nosebleed section. Jakyl played first, chainsaws in all. The lead singer got pissed off and threatened to kick the technician's ass because the speaker wasn't working right. There was a long break and then the lights went out and Aerosmith came on stage. The crowd went wild. The room was filled with an electric energy. Thousands of people were lost in it. We were the music. Anything goes was the attitude. I felt important and bigger than life. I couldn't believe I was in the same room at Steven Tyler and

Joe Perry. I looked from the TV screen to the band below. I'd seen them on TV before, but seeing them in person was just awesome.

July 13, 1995   Hole

I invited Jason to go to Lollapalooza with me. Nikki had mentioned going, which gave me the idea to call invite Jason. It was my way of paying Jason back for taking me to Cedar Point last month. I got up at 8am and got ready. I picked Jason up and then got my check at Interim. We headed to Columbus in my car. We stopped for lunch at Subway and got to Polaris at 1pm. We were only allowed to take in a water bottle and whatever you could fit in your pockets. We sat down on the grass once inside. It was crowded and we saw all kinds of people there. There were people with bright red, yellow, green and purple hair. I saw noses, ears, eyebrows, navels and nipples pierced. There were guys and girls with short hair and long hair. I saw lots of tattoos too. There was slam dancing and mosh pits. I saw people smoking cigarettes and pot both. We heard the Mighty, Mighty Bosstones, Jesus Lizard, Sinead O'Connor, Pavement, Cyprus Hill, Beck and Hole. I bought a bead necklace, Peace and Question Reality bumper stickers. I bought a T-Shirt. Almost bought some Ecstasy. On the side stage we saw Cocktails and then Geraldine Fibers. There was also a hickey and spanking contest! We got cooled off in the mist tents and drank lots of water since it was over 100 degrees that day! Despite my splitting headache, I never felt so alive! And Jason was great company.

May 18, 1996 Buzzard Fest

I got up early and got ready. Jason picked me up and we left for the Buzzardfest. We got lost, so we were an hour late arriving at the Blossom Music Center outside of Akron. It was bigger than Polaris and there were lots of Punks there. Jason was happy that he got a copy of Dr. Judy's book and got it signed by her and Jagger (From Love Phone's Radio Show!) I was happy I got my T-Shirt. We saw Goldfinger, Dash Rip Rock, Holy Barbarians, Tragically Hip, Universal Honey, Fast Action, Patti Rothburg, The Nixons and, best of all, No Doubt. I read Dr. Judy's book between bands. Missed Poe and Candlebox because we were both so tired and I had a splitting headache. We sat away from the music for a while, that is when we were lying against the tree. Then we drove home after that. (Stayed 2pm to 9pm). I felt sick and couldn't eat. I came home, showered, threw up and crawled into bed to sleep.

July 3, 1996 Infinite Sadness

We left at 5:15pm and stopped at McDonalds to eat. Jason took 61 South to 71 North, which took us about 25 miles out of our way. We hauled ass up to Cleveland and Jason drove like 100 miles an hour. We got to the Gund Arena about 8pm. Traffic was bad between the Indians Game and the concert. We searched for a parking spot and hurried inside. We only caught the last song or so of Garbage. There was a break and so we wandered around. We bought T-Shirts and found our

33

seats to watch The Smashing Pumpkins. They had cool music and a psychedelic background. The crowd was wild and we really enjoyed the concert. We left about 10:10pm. Traffic was horrendous. We waited 20 minutes in line just to get out of the area. Jason and I had a great talk on the way home about love, fears, cars, dreams, sex and kids.

August 23, 1996   Cranberries

Friday I got up and went to Jason's again. We got directions to Blossom Music Center and then laid down. Later, we cooked dinner—pasta. Then we left for the concert. We got there, parked and bought a T-shirt and poster and then sat down. Cracker came on. They were pretty cool. Then the Cranberries came on and the crowd went wild. I hopped and bopped around. Jason and I sang and kissed. We really got into the music. They did 4 encores. We left at 10:30pm, but didn't even leave the parking lot until 11:15am. Stopped for pizza in Akron. Large Peperoni for $6.00! Gas station for pop. Took 77 to 76 to 224 to 598 home. Because we were both tired the drive seem to take longer than the drive to Iowa. Got home at 2:30am.

August 23, 1997 Lollapalooza Two

Strolling among the vendors, listening the DJ and signing petitions, dirty dancing while watching the stage and kissing on the grassy knoll. The day at Lollapalooza was wonderful and the week that followed pretty cool too. It was very much a change from the week before it. Sunday I picked Jason up and we went to Paula's baby shower. We talked and ate and left after about 45 minutes. Then we went to the concert. We saw the Eels, then walked around and shopped. We ate and then watched Korn. Up on the hill Jason and I made out. Then we watched Tool and Prodigy. The Prodigy were weird, but kicked ass nonetheless. They had lights and smoke to an awesome beat. Jason and I dirty danced to them. Then we left Polaris. We came home and got ready for bed.

August 15, 1997 Secret Samadhi

I picked Jason up at 5:30. We went to his house and then Blossom Music Center. We walked around and listened to Mandrake and Luscious Jackson. Then we sat in our seats for LIVE. They had a cool temple set. There was lights and smoke. We knew most of the songs. It was a cool show, all except for beer being dumped on us. We kissed and hugged and danced a little together. Tired, we left. We ran out of gas between Ashland and Mansfield at 12:30am. Had to call a tow truck. The tow truck came at 1:10am and we had to pay $70 for 2 gallons of gas. We had to pay him once we got back to Jason's house at 1:45am. I got to my house at 2:15 and fell asleep.

Music Catalogue

2001

CD's Cari's

Christina Aguilera

Jessica Simpson

Amber

Smashing Pumpkins: Melancholy

Angelfish

Stabbing Westward: Wither

Mariah Carey

Sunscream: 03

Mariah Carey: Emotions

Mariah Carey: Daydream

Mariah Carey: Butterfly

The Corrs: Talking On Corners

Crystal Method: Vegas

Paula Cole: This Fire

Daft Punk: Homework

Dido: No Angel

Die Krupps: Rings of Steel

Doors: Best of

Melissa Ethridge: Your Little Secret

Faithless

Elisa Fiorillo: I Am

Garbage

Garbage: 2.0

Go Soundtrack

Whitney Houston's Greatest Hits

Jane Jenson: Comic book whore

Lestat: Vision of Sorrows

Jennifer Lopez: On the 6th

Madonna: Ray of Light

Sarah McLaughlin: Surfacing

Tara Mclean: Passenger

Debra Morgan

Alanis Morrisette: Jagged Little Pill

Alanis Morrisette: Supposed Infatuation Junkie

No Doubt: Return To Saturn

Once Were Warriors Sntrk

One: Jevan Comp

Pink: Can't Take Me Home

Poe: Haunted

Rammstien: Hunger

Republica

Shakespeare's Sister: Hormonally Yours

CDs: Jason's

Digital comes to life

Presidents of USA

Alternative NRG

Red Hot Chili Peppers: Blood

Ass Ponies

Pure Moods

Arrested Development: Zingalmundi

Primus: Frizzle Fry

Arrested Development: 3 days....

Primus: Miscellaneous Debris

Beavis and Butthead experience

Primus: Pork Soda

Beck: Mellow Gold

Primus: Sailing the Seas

Brian Seltzer Orchestra

Primus: Sausage

Bush: Sixteen Stone

Primus: Tales From The Punch

Cherry Poppin Daddies

Talking Heads: Sand 1&2

Cranberries: No Need

Three Doors Down

Cranberries: Everybody else

Underworld: dubnobasswithmy

Sheryl Crow: Tues. Nite

Violent Femms: Add it

Crash Test Dummies

Ween: Pure Guava

Dead Kennedys: Plastic/God

Weezer

DJ Magic Mike—Bass

Turn it Up and Pass it On

DJ DB: Drum and Bass Journey

Yes: Talk

Collective Soul--hints and allegations

Sampler: Alternative

Doors--Waiting for the sun

Sampler: Classical

Exploding Boy

Sample: R&B

Filter--short bus

Flaming lips--Satellite heart

Four NonBlonds--Bigger, Better

God Lives Underwater--Empty

Godsmack

Greenday--Dookie, Insomniac

Led Zeppelin--2

Live: Mental jewelry

Live: Throwing Copper

Metalica: Load

Marilyn Manson: American Family

Meatbeat Manifesto

Best of New Order

Nin: Broken

Nin: Downward Spiral

Nin: Further down the Spiral

Nin: Pretty Hate Machine

Nirvana: Nevermind

Nirvana: Unplugged in NY

No Doubt: Tragic Kingdom

Poe: Hello

Cari's Tapes	Jason's Tapes
Paula Abdul: Spellbound	The Clash: London Calling
Ace of Base: The sign	The Clash: Best of
Angel: The Last Dance	The Clash: The Story
The B52s: Cosmic Thing	Dead Kennedys: Fresh Fruit
Toni Braxton Mix	*DKs: Plastic,* Give me,
Braveheart Soundtrack	Dead Kennedys: Democracy
Mariah Carey: Daydream	Dead Kennedys: Christ
Mariah Carey: B-Sides	Doors: Waiting for the sun
Mariah Carey: Emotions	Joan Jet: Up your ally
Mariah Carey: Christmas	Mojo Nixon: Bo-da-shush
Sheryl Crow--Sheryl Crow/Globe	Metallica--garage band days
The Crow Soundtrack	Nirvana: In Utero
Belinda Carlisle: Runaway Horses	Ramones: All That
Paula Cole: This Fire/Amen	Ramones: End of
The Damned: part 2	Ramones: Half way
Delite: World Cliché	Ramones: Mania
Doors: Best of/The Doors	Sex Pistol: Nevermind the
Bullock Echo and the Bunnymen	Was not was: What's up
Expose: Exposure	
Garbage	
Debbie Gibson: Best of	
Gothik comp	
Grateful Dead: Best of	
Greenday: Dookie	

Heart: Bad Animals/Best of

Hole: live through this

Jewel: Pieces of you and Spirit Combo

Janet Jackson: janet/velvet rope

Jem and the holograms

Kokopelie Wind

La Bouche

Legend of the Blues

Lestat: Grave Desires

Lestat: Vision of Sorrows

Madonna: collection

Madonna: Erotica

Madonna: Ray of Light

Sarah McLaughlin---Fumbling toward Ecstasy/Surfacing

Lorena McKennett---Mask and Mirror/Journey

Mouth Music--Gaelic, African

Nirvana: Nevermind/ Unplugged

*No Doubt: Tragic Kingdom/Return To Satur*n

Offspring: Smash

Offspring: Ixnay on the Ombre

Liz Phair: American Thighs

Phish: Billy Breathless

Rainbowbright

Romeo and Juliet: soundtrack

The Saint: Soundtrack

Selena: Dreaming of you

Patty Smyth

TLC: Craxysexycool

Type O Negative

Book of roses

Verruca Salt

Swing (Brain Seltzer, Cherry)

Compilations

American Pie (50's and 60's)

Wild Thing (60's and 70's)

Dazed (1970's)

Manic (mid 80s)

Summer Rain (87-88)

Free (88-89)

Patience (1990-1991)

Emotions (1991-93)

Funky (90-95)

Stay (1993)

Secret (1994)

Thee Edge (1995)

Ironic (1996)

Crush (1996)

Insomnia (1997)

Smooth (1997)

Crazy (1998)

Paranoid (1998)

Down (1999)

Defiant (2000)

Higher (2000)

Wild (2001)

Odds and Ends

Night Club	Indiana Jones
Candlelight	Interviews 1&2
Love Hurts	Cities of Gold
Club Mix	
Dance	
Revolution	
Teen Spirit	
Only Happy When It Rains	
Dr. Demento	
Best of Punk	
Themes	
Fantasy (New Age)	
Echoes	
Around the World	
Germany	
France	
Global Meditation	

Compilations

Xanadu 1977-1982

Ramblin' Man by Allman Brothers

The Gambler by Kenny Rogers

Heartache Tonight by The Eagles

Gypsy by Fleetwood Mac

All Out of Love by Air Supply

I Love A Rainy Night by Eddie Rabbit

My Sharona by The Knack

Hit Me with Your Best Shot by Pat Benatar

Hey Mickey by Toni Basil

Physical by Olivia Newton John

Funkytown by Lipps Inc

Queen of Hearts by Juice Newton

Bettie Davis Eyes by Kim Karnes

Xanadu by Olivia Newton John

Making Love Out of Nothing At All by Air Supply

The Rose by Bette Middler

Lady by Kenny Rogers

Manic 1982 to 1986

Video Killed The Radio Star by The Bugles

Head Over Heels by The Go-Go's

Girls Just Wanna Have Fun by Cyndi Lauper

Everybody Have Fun Tonight by Wang Chung

Hungry Like The Wolf by Duran Duran

Something About You by Level 42

Obsession by Animation

Tainted Love by Soft Cell

I Just Died In Your Arms Tonight by Foreigner

Everybody Wants to Rule The World by Tears for Fears

Burn by the Talking Heads

Lips Are Sealed by The Go-Go's

I Know What Boys Like by The Waitresses

Melt With You by Modern English

Broken Wings by Mister Mister

Heart of Glass by Blondie

Borderline by Madonna

Manic Monday by The Bangles

Soundtrack To The 80s

Fame by Irena Cara

Flashdance by Irena Carey

Maniac by Michael Sembello

Imagination by Laura Braningan

Footloose by Kenny Logins

Holding Out For A Hero by Bonnie Tyler

Almost Paradise by Anne Wilson

Let's Hear It For The Boys by Denise Williams

Purple Rain by Prince

When Dove's Cry by Prince

Danger Zone by Kenny Logins

Hot Summer Nights by Miami Sound Machine

Take My Breath Away by Berlin

Glory of Love by Bette Middler

Underneath The Boardwalk by Bette Middler

The Wind Beneath My Wings by Bette Middler

Somewhere Out There by Linda Ronstadt and James Ingram

Mad 1986-1987

Only In My Dreams by Debbie Gibson

Mad About You by Belinda Carlisle

I Wanna Dance by Whitney Houston

Into the Groove by Madonna

Cruel Summer by Bananarama

Self-Control by Laura Braningan

Sweet Dreams by The Eurhythmics

Walk Like An Egyptian by The Bangles

Jessie James by Cher

I Get Weak by Belinda Carlisle

Time After Time by Cyndi Lauper

Season's Change by Expose

Live To Tell by Madonna

I Found Someone by Cher

Take My Breath Away by Berlin

Total Eclipse of the Heart by Bonnie Tyler

Heaven 1987-1988

Heaven's A Place On Earth by Belinda Carlisle

These Dreams by Heart

Didn't We Almost Have It All by Whitney Houston

I've Had The Time of My Life by Diane Warren

She's Like the Wind by Patrick Swayze

Hungry Eyes by Eric Carmen

If I Could Turn Back Time by Cher

Wind Beneath My Wings by Bette Midler

Summer of 69 by Bryan Adams

Free Falling by Tom Petty

Circle in The Sand by Belinda Carlisle

Forever Your Girl by Paula Abdul

Toy Soldiers by Martika

Eternal Flame by The Bangles

Heaven by Bryan Adams

Summer Rain 1988-1989

Leave the Light On by Belinda Carlisle

Ilsa Bonita by Madonna

Here Comes the Rain by The Eurhythmics

Every Breath You Take by The Police

What's Love Got To Do With It by Tina Turner

Foolish Beat by Debbie Gibson

Show Me Love by Foreigner

Right Here Waiting by Richard Marx

Always by Atlantic Star

Nothing's Going To Stop Us by Starship

Like A Prayer by Madonna

Keep Me Hanging On by Kim Wilde

With Or Without You by U2

Hold On To The Nights by Richard Marx

Naturally 80s/90s Dance

Venus by Bananarama

Locomotion why Kylie Minogue

Into the Groove by Madonna

I Wanna Dance by Whitney Houston

Come Go With Me by Expose

I Can't Wait by Nu Shooz

Naturally by Sheena Easton

This Time I Know It's For Read Donna Summer

Real Love by Jodi Watley

Nasty by Janet Jackson

Monie, Monie by Billy Idol

Wild Thing by Tone Loc

Pump Up The Jam by Technetronic

Just A Touch of Love by C&C Music Factory

Good Vibrations by Marky Mark

Back II Life by Soul II Soul

Like A Prayer by Madonna

Patience (Big Hair Bands) 80s/90s

Patience by Guns and Roses

November Rain by Guns and Roses

Every Rose Has Its Thorn by Poison

Janie's Got A Gun by Aerosmith

Shook Me All Night Long by AC/DC

Back in Black by AC/DC

You Give Love A Bad Name by Bon Jovi

Livin; On A Prayer by Bon Jovi

When I See You Smile by Bad English

Price of Love by Bad English

When The Children Cry by White Lion

Winds of Change by The Scorpions

The Unforgiven by Metallica

Take Me Home Tonight 80s

Paradise City by Guns and Roses

Pour Some Sugar on Me by Def Leopard

Here I Go Again by White Snake

Heaven by Warrant

High Enough by Damn Yankees

Take Me Home Tonight by Eddie Monie

Bring On The Heartbreak by Def Leopard

Living On A Prayer by Bon Jovi

Every Rose Has A Thorn by Poison

When I See You Smile by Bad English

Miles Away by Winger

Is This Love by Winger

When The Children Cry by White Lion

Patience by Guns and Roses

Price of Love by Bad English

Rush 1990

Waiting For A Star To Fall by Boy Meets Girl

If Wishes Came True by Sweet Sensation

I Sill Believe by Brenda K Starr

Vision of Love by Mariah Carey

All The Man I Need by Whitney Houston

Save The Best For Last by Vanessa Williams

All I Wanna Do by Heart

Express Yourself by Madonna

Love and Understanding by Cher

On The Way Up by Ilsa Foriello

Promise of a New Day by Paula Abdul

In This House by Traci Spencer

Tell Me Why by Expose

Rush, Rush by Paula Abdul

Love Takes Time by Mariah Carey

How Can I Ease the Pain by Lisa Fischer

Too Sexy 1991-1992

Let's Talk About Sex by Salt N Pepa

I Wanna Sex You Up by Color Me Badd

I Touch Myself by The Divinyls

U Can't Touch This by MC Hammer

I'm Too Sexy by Right Said Fred

Ice Ice Baby by Vanilla Ice

Baby Got Back by Sir Mix A lot

Gonna Make You Sweat by C&C Music Factory

3Am Eternal by KLF

Informer by Snow

Jump Around by House of Pain

2 Legit to Quit by MC Hammer

Set Adrift in the Memory of Bliss by PM Dawn

Unbelievable by EMF

Right Here, Right Now by Jesus Jones

Grove is In The Heart by Dee Lite

My Lovin (You're Never Gonna Get It) by En Vogue

Justify My Love by Madonna

Everything 1992

Everything I Do by Bryan Adams

I'll Be There by Mariah Carey

This Used To Be My Playground by Madonna

Love Shack by B52's

The Way That You Love Me by Paula Abdul

Save Up All Your Tears by Cher

Winds of Change by Scorpions

Price of Love by Bad English

To Be With You by Mr. Big

More Than Words by Extreme

Endless Summer Nights by Richard Marx

If You Asked Me To by Celine Dion

Miracle by Whitney Houston

Heaven by Bryan Adams

Said I Love You But I Lied by Michael Bolton

Undone 1993

Ordinary World by Duran Duran

The Power of Love by Celine Dion

Do I Have To Say The Words by Bryan Adams

Just For Tonight by Vanessa Williams

Can't Let Go by Mariah Carey

Sometimes Love Just Ain't Enough by Patty Smyth

Alone by Heart

Deeper and Deeper by Madonna

Come Undone by Duran Duran

You Think of Me by Mariah Carey

That's The Way Love Goes by Janet Jackson

Runaway Train by Soul Asylum

Miles Away by Winger

I'll Never Get Over You (Getting Over Me) by Expose

Water From The Moon by Celine Dion

Shine by Patty Smyth

Red Light 90s R&B

Red Light by TLC

Any Time, Any Place by Janet Jackson

I'll Make Love To You by Boyz II Men

Never Gonna Let You Go by Tina M

Superwoman by Karen White

Back To Life by Soul II Soul

Motown Philly by Boyz II Men

Bop Hop by Brooklyn

No Diggity by Backstreet

Here Comes The Hotstepper by Ina Comoze

Tell Me Why by Expose

Breathe Again by Toni Braxton

Killing Me Softly by the Fugies

How Can I Ease The Pain by Lisa Fischer

Again by Janet Jackson

Stay 1994 Spring

I Will Always Love You by Whitney Houston

Black Velvet by Alannah Miles

Damn, I Wish I Was Your Lover by Sophie B Hawkins

Dreams by The Cranberries

Everything Fades Away by Mariah Carey

Stay by Shakespeare's Sister

All That She Wants by Ace of Base

Because The Night by 10,000 Maniacs

Linger by the Cranberries

The Woman In Me by Heart

Come To My Window by Melissa Ethridge

Without You by Mariah Carey

Rain by Madonna

Strong Enough by Sheryl Crow

These Are the Days by 10,000 Maniacs

Secret 1994-1995

Will You Be There (In the Morning) by Heart

Bed of Roses by Bon Jovi

Color of the Night by Laura

Far Behind by Candlebox

Human Nature by Madonna

Until The End of Time by Foreigner

I Believe In Love by Elton John

Always by Bon Jovi

Rain by Janet Jackson

Secret by Madonna

Creep by TLC

Sitting In My Room by Brandi

Now I Lay Me Down Sophie B Hawkins

Hey Jealousy by The Gin Blossoms

Ecstasy by Rusted Root

The Edge 1995 Summer

Come As You Are by Nirvana

Jeremy by Pearl Jam

Stars by Hum

I Got A Girl by Tripping Daisy

Loser by Beck

Lump by Presidents of the USA

Come Down by Bush

Changes by Candlebox

Interstate Love Song by Stone Temple Pilots

Doll Parts by Hole

Take A Bow by Madonna

I'm The Only One by Melissa Ethridge

You Outta Know by Alanis Morrisette

Connection by Elastica

Here and Now by Letters to Cleo

Buddy Holly by Weezer

New Age Girl by Deadeye Dick

Zombies by The Cranberries

Lightening Crashes by Live

Rain 1995 Fall

November Rain by Guns and Roses

Bedtime by Madonna

Fantasy by Mariah Carey

What is Love by Haddaway

Another Night by The Real McCoy

Where Did You Go by La Bouche

Seether by Verruca Salt

Come Out And Play by The Offspring

When I Come Around by Greenday

Sodajerk by Buffalo Tom

No Rain by Blind Melon

What's Up by The Four Non-Blonds

Closer To Free by The Bodeans

How Do You Talk To An Angel by the Heights

Waterfalls by TLC

Kiss From A Rose by Seal

One Sweet Day by Mariah Carey

Make It Home by Julianna Hatfield

Angst 1995-1996

Self-Esteem by The Offspring

Basket Case by Greenday

Undone by Weezer

Suffocate Me by Angelfish

Violet by Hole

Blackhole Sun by Soundgarden

Closer by Nine Inch Nails

Three Little Pigs by Green Jelly

Wynonna's Big Brown Beaver by Primus

Possum Kingdom by The Toadies

Piranha by Tripping Daisy

What's Up by The Four Nonblonds

Today by Smashing Pumpkins

When I Come Around by Greenday

Come Out And Play by The Offspring

Plush by Stone Temple Pilots

I Alone by Live

Me and a Gun by Tori Amos

Ironic 1996

One of Us by Joan Osborne

Who Will Save Your Soul by Jewel

Ironic by Alanis Morrisette

I Wanna Come Over by Melissa Ethridge

Just A Girl by No Doubt

Only Happy When It Rains by Garbage

Angry Johnny by Poe

Be My Lover by La Bouche

Ready to Go by Republica

Pepper by The Butthole Surfers

Sister by The Nixons

Here In Your Bedroom by Goldfinger

Counting Blue Cars by Dishwalla

Banditos by Refreshments

I Kissed A Girl by Jill Souble

Lovefool by The Cardigans

I'm In Chains by Tina Arena

Only Love by Sophie Hawkins

Nobody 1996 Fall

Liar by The Cranberries

Queer by Garbage

Girl Like You

Scooby Snacks by The Fun Lovin' Criminals

Trigger Happy Jack by Poe

Novocain For The Soul by The Eels

Bullet With Butterfly Wings by The Smashing Pumpkins

More Human Than Human by Rob Zombie

Pretty Piece of Flesh by

I Had A Dream by The Butthole Surfers

Shame by Stabbing Westward

Guilty by Gravity Kills

God Lives Underwater by God Lives Under Water

Cowgirl by Underworld

Caught a Light Sneeze by Tori Amos

Down By The Water by PJ Harvey

Nobody Loves Me (Like You Do)

Milk by Garbage

Crush 1996-1997

Hello by Poe

Sweet Dreams by La Bouche

Oo Ahh by Gina G

This Is The Night by Amber

C'mon Ride The Train by Quad City DJs

You're Makin Me High by Toni Braxton

If It Makes You Happy by Sheryl Crow

You Were Meant For Me by Jewel

Unbreak My Heart by Toni Braxton

Don't Speak by No Doubt

When I Saw You by Mariah Carey

#1 Crush by Garbage

Don't Let Go by En Vogue

Possession by Sarah MacLauchlan

St Teresa by Joan Osborne

I Miss You When You're Gone by The Cranberries

Broken Phone Booth by Primitive Radio Gods

Insomnia 1997

Lakini's Juice by Live

1979 by The Smashing Pumpkins

Volcano Girls by Verruca Salt

The Perfect Drug by Nine Inch Nails

I Could Never Be Your Woman by Whitetown

Lucas With The Lid Off by Lucas

Insomnia by Faithless

Pearl's Girl by Underworld

Bitch by Meredith Brooks

I Want You by Savage Garden

Underground by Sneaker Pimps

Out Of My Mind by Duran Duran

Heaven by The Offspring

Pressure by Sunscream

Where Have All The Cowboys Gone by Paula Cole

Sunny Came Home by Shawn Colvin

Foolish 1997

I'm Not An Addict by K's Choice

Hole in My Soul by Aerosmith

To The Moon and Back by Savage Garden

Building A Mystery by Sarah MacLauchlan

I Don't Wanna Wait by Paula Cole

Foolish Games by Jewel

More Than I Can by Jane Jensen

High by Jimmy's Chicken Shack

Don't Want You by Luna Chicks

Trip Like I Do by Crystal Method

I and I by Tajia Seville

Naked Eye by Luscious Jackson

Forest For The Trees by Dream

Walkin' On The Sun by Smash Mouth

Tubthumping by Chumbawumba

Hitchin; A Ride by Greenday

Knock On Wood by The Mighty Mighty Bosstones

Revolution 1997-1998 Electronica

Underground by Sneaker Pimps

Insomnia by Faithless

Pearl Girl by Underworld

Oil by Moby

Guilty by Juno Reactor

Keep Hope Alive by The Crystal Method

Right Here, Right Now by Fat Boy Slim

Love Island by Fat Boy Slim

Red Alert by Basement Jaxx

Block Rocking Beats by The Chemical Brothers

Full Throttle by Prodigy

Oh by Underworld

Breathe by Prodigy

A Final Hit by Left Field

Crazy 1998

Revolution 909 by Daft Punk

From Your Mouth by God Lives Under Water

Ray of Light by Madonna

Push It by Garbage

Breakdown by Mariah Carey

3am by Matchbox 20

Sex and Candy by Marcy's Playground

Shanti/Ashanti by Madonna

Crazy by Plumb

Whatever by Aimee Mann

Legend of a Cowgirl by Imani Coppola

Clumsy by Our Lady of Peace

Sherry Frazier by Marcy's Playground

Flagpole Sitta by Harvey Danger

Push by Matchbox 20

Save Yourself by Stabbing Westward

When I Grow UP by Garbage

DA DA DA by Trio (German)

Torn 1998

Sweet Surrender by Sarah MacLauchlan

My All by Mariah Carey

Torn by Natalie Imbruglia

Frozen by Madonna

Walk This Earth Alone by Laura Christy

Kiss The Rain by Billie Myers

32 Flavors by Alana Davis

I Do by Lisa Loeb

All Cried Out by Allure

This Boy Is Mine by Monica and Brandi

What Would Happen If by Meredith Brooks

My Heart Will Go On by Celine Dion

Butterfly by Mariah Carey

Truly, Madly, Deeply by Savage Garden

You're Still The One by Shania Twain

Together Again by Janet Jackson

Silver Lining by Jewel

Paranoid 1998

Spark by Tori Amos

Uninvited by Alanis Morrisette

Kiss The Rain by Billie Myers

The Power of Goodbye by Madonna

I Get Lonely by Janet Jackson

Ava Adore by The Smashing Pumpkins

Du Hast by Rammstien

I Think I'm Paranoid by Garbage

Celebrity Skin by Hole

Crush by Jennifer Paige

Cruel Summer by Ace of Base

Today by Poe

Life In Mono by Mono

Jump Jive and Wail by Brian Seltzer

Zuit Suit Riot by Cherry Poppin' Daddy's

My Favorite Mistake by Sheryl Crow

Save Tonight by Eagle Eye Cherry

The Way by Fastball

One Week by The Bare Naked Ladies

Down 1999

Unpretty by TLC

If You Had My Love by Jenifer Lopez

Nothing Really Matters by Madonna

Special by Garbage

Maria by Blondie

New by No Doubt

Anything but Down by Sheryl Crow

Down So Long by Jewel

If I Fall by Tara McLean

Angel by Sarah MacLauchlan

Angels Would Fall by Melissa Ethridge

From This Moment On by Shania Twain

Troubled The Way by Natalie Imbruglia

Here With Me by Dido

Runaway by The Corrs

I Sill Believe by Mariah Carey

 Will Remember You by Sarah MacLauchlan

Believe 1999

Believe by Cher

Genie in a Bottle by Christina Aguilera

Livin' La Vida Loca by Ricky Martin

Bailamous by Enrique Iglesias

Waiting For Tonight by Jennifer Lopez

Believer by BT

Right Here, Right Now by Fat Boy Slim

Beautiful Stranger by Madonna

Pretty Fly (For A White Guy) by The Offspring

Sweetheart by Mariah Carey

No Scrubs by TLC

Thank U by Alanis Morrisette

Hands by Jewel

Spanish Eyes by Ricky Martin

No Me Ames by Jennifer Lopez and Marc Anthony

Revolution 1999-2000 Electronica

Blade by The Crystal Method

Ready, Steady, Go by Paul Oakenfold

Born Slippy by Underworld

Absurd by Fluke

Days Go By by Dirty Vegas

Believer by BT

Defiant by Christopher Lawrence

Adagio for Strings by Orbit

Higher by Techno Sonique

Natural Blues by Moby

Around the World by ATC

Around The World by Daft Punk

Desire 2000

With Arms Wide Open by Creed

Crash and Burn by Savage Garden

Turn To You by Christina Aguilera

Object of my Desire by Amber

He Wasn't Man Enough by Toni Braxton

So Young by The Corrs

Be With You by Mandy Moore

Breathe by Faith Hill

Did You Ever by Jessica Simpson

Spanish Guitars by Toni Braxton

Simple Kind of Life by No Doubt

So Sad To Stay by The Mighty Mighty Bosstones

Wasted by Smash Mouth

Higher by Creed

Adajio For Strings by Orbit

Desert Rose by Sting

Music by Madonna

Sexual by Amber

Defiant 2000 Summer

Poor Boy by Tara MacLean

She Wants You by Billie

What A Girl Wants by Christian Aguilera

Ex-Girlfriend by No Doubt

Natural Blues by Moby

Then The Morning Comes by Smash Mouth

Smooth by Santana

American Pie by Madonna

The Chemicals Between Us by Bush

Take My Picture by Filter

Dolphin's Cry by Live

The World Is Not Enough by Garbage

Moment of Weakness by Bif Naked

Defiant by Christopher Lawrence

Higher by Techno Sonique

I Knew I Love You

I Want To Love You Forever by Jessica Simpson

Wild 2000-2001

Breathless by The Corrs

Come On Over by Christina Aguilera

The Way The You Love Me by Faith Hill

Don't Tell Me by Madonna

Most Girls by Pink

Gotta Tell You by Samantha Mumba

Dance With Me by Debra Morgan

Faded by Soul Decision

Love Don't Cost A Thing by Jennifer Lopez

Artificial Sweetener by No Doubt

Wild by Poe

Kryptonite by 3 Doors Down

South Side by Moby and Gwen Stefani

Around the World by ATC

He Took Her To A Movie by Lady Tron

Who Let The Dogs Out by the Baha Men

Original Prankster by The Offspring

The Itch by Vitamin C

You Make Me Sick by Pink

Silence 2001

Silence by Sarah MacLauchlan

Only Time by Enya

Tonight and The Rest of My Life by Nina Gordon

Cup of Coffee by Garbage

Mirror, Mirror by M2M

Underneath Your Clothes by Shakira

Misery by Pink

Love Is Alive by Joan Osborne

True Friends by Shannon Curfman

Don't Let Me Get Me by Pink

Wherever, Whenever by Shakira

Carino by Jennifer Lopez

Righteous Love by Joan Osborne

Precious Illusions by Alanis Morrisette

Silence Remix by Sarah MacLauchlan

Irresistible 2001 Summer

Again by Lenny Kravitz

Jaded by Aerosmith

Hemorrhage by Fuel

Drive by Incubus

Play by Jennifer Lopez

Free by Mya

Survivor by Destiny's Child

Lady Marmalade by Christina, Pink and Mya

Hey Pretty by Poe

Can't Fight The Moonlight by Leanne Rimes

Hunter by Dido

Irresistible by The Corrs

Irresistible by Jessica Simpson

Not A Virgin by Poe

In My Pocket by Mandy

Castles In the Sky by Ian Van Dahl

Someone To Call My Lover by Janet Jackson

Everywhere by Michelle Branch

I'm A Believer by Smash Mouth

Nobody Wants To Be Lonely by Ricky Martin
                    And Christina Aguilera

Steady 2001-2002

Rock Steady by No Doubt

Give Me A Reason by The Corrs

Through the Rain by Mariah Carey

Fallin' by Alicia Keys

Hit 'em Up Style by Blue

Cherry Lips (Go Baby Go) by Garbage

I Wanna Be Bad by Willa Ford

I Wanna Be in Love by Melissa Ethridge

Wrong Impression by Natalie Imbruglia

Standing Still by Jewel

Hands Clean by Alanis Morrisette

Ain't It Funny by Jennifer Lopez

Get The Party Started by Pink

Ready, Steady, Go by Paul Oakenfold

Did Ya Understand That by Willa Ford

Hey Baby by No Doubt

Cry Baby by Jamie Lynn Sigler

Rapture 2002 Trance

Believe From Run Lola Run

Rapture by Iio

I See Stars by Robin Fox

Heaven by DJ Sammy

Touch Me by Rui DaSilver

Toca's Miracle by Fragma

Only You by Sulk

Ayla II by Ayla

Flowers Duet by Jonathan Peters

Sandstorm by Darude

Omnibus by Lautspecher with Katie Skate

Can't Keep Me Silent by Angelic

I See Right Through You

Look At Us by Sarina Paris

Castles in the Sky by Ivana Van Dahl

Will I by Ivana Van Dahl

Ordinary World by Aurora

Rapture (Techno Remix) by Iio

Dirty 2002-2003

Lifestyles of the Rich and Famous by Good Charlotte

Sk8er Boi by Avril Lavigne

Dirty by Christina Aguilera

Die Another Day by Madonna (James Bond)

I'm Gonna Getcha Good by Shania Twain

Jenny From The Block by Jennifer Lopez

Just Like A Pill by Pink

She F*$%ing Hates Me by Puddle of Mud

Papa Don't Preach by Kelly Osborne

Hero by Chad Kroger

Game of Love by Michelle Branch

I'm Jealous by Shania Twain

Beautiful by Christina Aguilera

A Moment Like This by Kelly Clarkson

A Sort of Fairy Tale by Tori Amos

Landslide by The Dixie Chicks

Cry by Faith Hill

I'm With You by Avril Lavigne

Family Portrait by Pink

Paint's Peeling by Rilo Kelly

Burn 2003

Bring Me To Life by Evanescence

All The Things She Said by tatu

Intuition by Jewel

Burn For You by Kreo

Fighter by Christina Aguilera

Losing My Grip by Avril Lavigne

I'm Glad by Jennifer Lopez

Miss Independent by Kelly Clarkson

Bring On The Heartache by Mariah Carey

Swing by The All American Rejects

Too Bad by Nickleback

Here Without You by 3 Doors Down

Heaven by Live

Why Can't I by Liz Phair

White Flag by Dido

Hollywood by Madonna

Unwell by Matchbox 20

Are You Happy Now by Michelle Branch

I Don't Give A Damn by Avril Lavigne

Fallen 2003-2004

Fallen by Sarah MacLauchlan

Stand by Jewel

First Cut by Sheryl Crow

Someday by Nickleback

Stacey's Mom by Fountains of Wayne

God Is DJ by Pink

Boys of Summer by The Atari's

Forever and Always by Shania Twain

Baby I Love You by Jennifer Lopez

Voice Within by Christina Aguilera

Detective by No Doubt

Milkshake by Kellis

Zion by Fluke

Dread Rock by Oakenfold

Behind Blue Eyes by Limp Bizket

My Immortal by Evanescence

Runaway by Live

It's My Life by No Doubt

Crazy in Love by Beyoncé

Stupid 2004

Breathe by Melissa Ethridge

Stupid by Sarah MacLauchlan

El Beso De Final by Christina Aguilera

Do You Want To Dance by Maya

Everything by Alanis Morrisette

Naughty Girl by Beyoncé

Good Boys by Blondie

Don't Leave Home by Dido

Breathe Your Name by Sixpence None The Richer

Light In Your Eyes by Sheryl Crow

Devils and Angels by Touby Lightman

World on Fire by Sarah MacLauchlan

Hit That by The Offspring

Girls and Boys by Good Charlotte

Away From the Sun by 3 Doors Down

I Want You by Thalia

Extraordinary by Liz Phair

More To Live by Stacie Orcio

Runaway by Hoobastank

Breakaway 2005

Because of You by Kelly Clarkson

Listen To Your Heart by DHT

Girl Next Door by Saving Jane

Good is Good

Since You've Been Gone by Kelly Clarkson

Photograph by Nickleback

Into the Light by Full Blown Rose

Rich Girl by Gwen Stefani

Pon de Reply by Rhianna

Switch by Will Smith

Hang Up by Madonna

Every time We Touch by Cascade

Listen To Your Heart by DHT Remix

Breakaway by Kelly Clarkson

Save Me by Saving Jane

Behind Hazel Eyes by Kelly Clarkson

Broken 2005 Fall

The Hand That Feeds by Nine Inch Nails

Why Do You Love Me by Garbage

TKO La Tigre

Coin Operated Boy by Dresden Dolls

Boulevard of Broken Dreams by Greenday

Broken by Seether and Amy Lee

Since You've Been Gone by Kelly Clarkson

He Wasn't by Avril Lavigne

1985 by Bowling For Soup

What Ya Been Waitin' For by Gwen Stefani

Hang On by Smash Mouth

Lady by Lenny Kravitz

Wake Me Up When September Ends by Greenday

Almost by Bowling For Soup

Lonely No More by Rob Thomas

Nobody's Home by Avril Lavigne

Man Who Sold The World by Jordis Unga

Now What by Lisa Marie Presley

The Good Rilo Kelly

Come On Closer by Jem

Good 2006

This Strange Effect by Hooverphonic

La Tortura by Shakira

Cool by Gwen Stefani

We Belong Together by Mariah Carey

Listen To You Your Heart by DHT

Behind These Hazel Eyes

Girl Like Me by Saving Jane

Behind These Hazel Eyes by Kelly Clarkson

Into the Light by Full Blown Rose

Photograph by Nickleback

Good is Good by Sheryl Crow

Pretty Vegas by JD from Inxs

Rumors by Lindsay Lohan

Rich Girl by Gwen Stefani

Pon De Reply by Rihanna

Switch by Will Smith

Hang Up by Madonna

Every Time We Touch Cascade

Listen To Your Heart Dance Mix by DHT

Because of You by Kelly Clarkson

Saving Me by Nickleback

Better 2006 (Redo of Good)

This Women's Work by Kate Bush

Keep Holding On by Avril Lavigne

Who Knew by Pink

Never Again by Kelly Clarkson

Better Than Me by Hinder

Pain by Paralyzer

Lose Control

Breathe

It's Not Over

If Everyone Cared by Chad Kroger

Makes Me Wonder

Say It Right by Nelly Furtado

Hot 2007

Good Enough by Evanescence

When You're Gone by Avril Lavigne

Bubbly by Colbie Calliet

Love Song

Love Is Free by Sheryl Crow

Into the Night by Santana Ft Chad Kroger

Island by Starting Line

Tell Me Where It Hurts by Garbage

Paralyzer by Finger Eleven

1-2-3 by Fiest

Hot by Avril Lavigne

Feedback by Janet Jackson

Amazing by Seal

Please Don't Stop The Music by Rhianna

Dance Like There is No Tomorrow by Paula Abdul

No One by Alicia Keys

Tattoo by Jordin Sparks

The Little Things by Colbie Calliet

Black Horse by Katie Tunstall

All Good Things by Nelly Furtado

Cold 2006-2007

Stupid Girls by Pink

Walk A Way by Kelly Clarkson

If Everyone Cared by Chad Kroger

Better Than Me by Hinder

Pain by Paralyzer

Cold by Crossfate

Cold by Evans Blue

Call Me When You Are Sober by Evanescence

How To Save A Life by The Fray

Better in Time by Leona Lewis

In My Arms by Plumb

This Woman's Work by Kate Bush

Lips of an Angel by Hinder

Hot and Cold by Katie Perry

Happy by 2008

In My Arms by Plumb

It's All For You by Leona Lewis

Hanging On by Cheyenne Kimball

Touch My Body by Mariah Carey

Clumsy by Fergie

No Air by Jordin Sparks

Psycho by Puddle of Mud

Feels Like Tonight by Daughtry

It's Not My Time by Three Doors Down

Falling Down by Atreyu

So Happy by Theory of a Dead Man

Rise Above This by Seether

One Original Thing by Cheyenne Kimball

Love Me by Alecia Keys

Baby Is A Butterfly by Joan Osborne

Bleeding Love by Leona Lewis

Damaged by Plumb and Sarah MacLauchlan

I Go Crazy by DHT

Dance 90s/00s

Get Into The Groove Madonna

Come Go With Me by Expose

Tonight is the Tonight by La Bouche

Where Do You Go by La Bouche

Rhythm of the Night by Corona

Young and Proud by Ace of Base

Hottstepper by Ina Camoze

Push It by Salt N Pepa

Scatman by Scatman

Lucas with The Lid Off by Lucas

Insomnia by Faithless

Love Island by Fat Boy Slim

I See Stars by Robin Fox

Rapture by Iio

You 2006-2013 Country & Pop

You by Tara McLean
Red by Taylor Swift
Just Give Me A Reason by Pink
Here's To Never Giving Up by Avril
Almost Home by Mariah Carey
Werewolf by Fiona Apple
Music in Me by Paula Cole
Satisfied by Jewel
Sooner or Later by Michelle Branch
We Are Never Getting Back Together by Taylor Swift
Cowboy Casanova by Carrie Underworld
Six Ways to Sunday by Blackberry
Ho Hey by the Lumineers
Into The Open Air from The Brave Soundtrack
Learn Me To The Right from The Brave Soundtrack
Never Alone by Lady Antebellum
I Was Here by Lady Antebellum

Dark 2011-2012 Rock & Gothic

Fade by Sad Alice Said

Blood For Poppies by Garbage

What You Want by Evanescence

Unbroken by Black Veil Brides

Trip the Darkness by Lacuna Coil

Whispers in the Dark by Skillet

Dark Lantern by Mantagora Scream

July by Katonia

Tear The World Down by We Are The Fallen

Among by Nox Arcana

Poison by Tanja Turunen

Mother of Light by Epica

Arise by Flyleaf

Awake and Alive by Skillet

Fallen Angels by Black Veil Brides

Battle in Me by Garbage

Losing My Religion by Lacuna Coil

A New Way To Bleed by Evanescence

Open Your Eyes by Said Alice Said

Cut 2011 Fall

Firework by Katy Perry

Perfect by Pink

Already Gone by Kelly Clarkson

Obsession by Skye Ferrera

ET by Katy Perry

Alejandro by Lady Gaga

Boom Boom Ba

Sleep Alone by Bat For Lashes

Cut by Plumb

Tore My Heart by Oona

Evelyn Evelyn

Sweet Dreams by Emily Browning

Part of Me by Katy Perry

Stronger by Kelly Clarkson

Big Girls Don't Cry by Fergie

Set Fire To The Rain by Adele

Wide Awake 2012 Summer

Lost in Paradise by Evanescence

Blow Me (One Last Kiss) by Pink

Looking Hot by Gwen Stefani

Your Body by Christina Aguilera

Catch My Breath by Kelly Clarkson

Lights (Remix) by Ellie Goulding

I Believe In Love by Lily Collins

Can You Save Me by Apple Trees and Tangerines

Open Your Eyes by Sad Alice Said

My Heart is Broke by Evanescence

Dark Side by Kelly Clarkson

Try by Pink

Settle Down by No Doubt

Brand New Day by Ryan Star

Sweet 2012-2013

Cruisin' by The Offspring

Give Me Your Lovin' by MIA

Born this Way by Lady Gaga

Bounce by Calvin Harris

Don't You Worry Child by Swedish House Mafia

Anything Could Happen by Ellie Goulding

Sweet Nothing by Calvin Harris

Judas by Lady Gaga

Turn Me On

Feels So Close

The Edge of Glory by Lady Gaga

Explosions by Ellie Goulding

Somebody I Used To Know

It Will Rain by Bruno Mars

Guardian by Alanis Morrisette

Another 2013

Everything At Once by Lenka

Rumor Has It by Adele

Dear Jenny by The Dresden Dolls

Not Far by Lily Allen

Sick of You by Cake

Days Go By by The Offspring

Rolling in the Deep by Adele

Girl on Fire by Alecia Keys

Right Here by Brandi

Receive by Alanis Morrisette

Happy Pills by Norah Jones

Hurry, Hurry by Jessie Baylen

King of Anything by Colbie Calliet

The Show by Lenka

Ho Hey by the Lumineers

Can't Stop Loving You

The Celestials by The Smashing Pumpkins

Tessellate 2013

Serpents by Sharon Van Etton

110% by Jessie Ware

Shake It Out by Florence and The Machine

My Devise by Ayria

Genesis by Grimes

Tessellate by Alt J

Boy by Ra Ra Riot

I Don᾽t Want To See You by Joy Formidable

Never Let Me Go by Florence and the Machine

Fitzepleasure by Alt J

Trojans by Atlas Genius

Austere by The Joy Formidable

Oblivion by Grimes

Heartlines by Florence and The Machine

Girl by Ayria

Shocked 2013-2014

22 by Lily Allen

Shock by Anja Tijoux

Roar by Katie Perry

Domino by Jessie J

Heart Attack by Demi Lovato

Applause by Lady Gaga

Come and Get It by Selena Gomez

#Beautiful by Mariah Carey

Clarity by Zedd

How's Never by Ivy

I Need Your Love by Calvin Harris and Ellie Goulding

Tonight by Collette

Siberia by Siberia

I'm Just Saying by Karmin

Radioactive

Blue Alice by Ayria

Running Fire by Eurobeat

Home 2013

Rose Tattoo by The Drop Kick Murphy's

Home by Phillip Philips

It's Time by Imagine Dragons

Friday I'll Be Over You by Allison Ireheta

Wear Me Out by Skyler Grey

Miss Disarray by Gin Blossoms

Easy Way Out by Goyte

My Songs Know What You Did by Fallout Boy

You Really Wake Up The Sprit by Duke Spirit

Feel Again by One Republic

Scars by Allison Ireheta

Breeze Blocks by Alt J

All Eyes by Imagine Dragons

Walking On Air by Kerli

In the End by The Black Veil Brides

Oblivion 2013 Fall

Oblivion by Bastille

Gone, Gone, Gone by Phillip Philips

Never Gonna Be Alone by Nickleback

She's So Sorry by Hedley

Rock and Roll by Avril Lavigne

I Love It by Icona Pop

American Girl by Bonnie McKee

It's My Party by Jessie J

Dark Horse by Katy Perry

My Kind of Love by Emile Sand

Come Along With Me by Tityo

Under Cover by Selena Gomez

True Love by Pink

Royals by Lorde

Brave by Sara Barillies

Summer Time Sadness by Luna Del Rey

Oblivion by Susan Sunford

Go 2014 Winter

Demons by Imagine Dragons

Best Day by America Authors

Wake Me Up by Avicii

Pumpin' Blood by Nonono

Let Her Go by Passenger

We Might Be Dead

Chocolate by 1975

Up In Flames by She Wants

On Top of the World by Imagine Dragons

Pompeii by Bastille

Come With Me by The Kongos

Love Don't Die by The Fray

Do I Want To Know by The Artic Monkeys

Please Ask For Help by Telekinesis

Still Into You by Paramour

Can't Remember To Forget You by Shakira

Do What Want by Lady Gaga

Burn by Ellie Goulding

Neon Lights by Demi Lovato

Last Love Song by ZZ Ward

Let It Go by Idina Menzel

Sail 2014 Spring

Sail by AWOL Nation

Whirring by Joy Formidable

Control by Garbage

So Close by Calvin Harris

Obsession by Sky Ferrera

Youth Knows No Pain Lykki Lei

Tear Drops on My Pillow by Dum Dum Girls

Girl Like Me by Lady Hawk

Lemon Scent by Dead Sara

First Light by My Morning Jacket

Does This Mean You Are Moving On

Got Some by Lykki Lei

Pumped Up Kicks by Foster The People

Up in Flames by She Wants Revenge

Guilty, Filthy Soul by AWOL Nation

Ready 2014 Summer

A Little Party by Fergie

Hello by Karmin

Happy by Pharell

Fancy by Iggy

Work by Britany Spears

Read For the Weekend by Icona Pop

You and I by Lady Gaga

Birthday by Katy Perry

About Us by Collette

I Follow Rivers by Lykki Lei

Stay the Night by Zedd

Glad You Came by The Wanted

Hey Brother by Avicii

Heartbeat by The Fray

Feel Again by One Republic

Things We Lost in the Fire by Bastille

Team by Lorde

West Coast by Lana Del Rey

Love Is The Drug

Summer 2014

We Remain by Christina Aguilera

Girls by Ingrid

All We Are by Pin

Dare by Shakira

I Want It by Karmin

Summer by Calvin Harris

Hidaway by Dzeko

Really Don't Care by Demi Lovato

Break Free by Ariana Grande

Hello Kitty by Avril Lavigne

Hard Out There by Lily Allen

Trouble's Lament

No Rest For the Wicked by Lykki Lei

I Choose You by Sara Barillies

In Your Shoes

Raging Fire by Phillip Phillips

Who We Are by Imagine Dragons

Maps by M5

I Forgive by Lacuna Coil

Emulator by The Crystal Method

Best 2014 Fall

I Am The Best by 2NE1

Hate To Love You by Karmin

Hot Air Balloon by Lilly Allen

Boom Clap by Charlie XCX

All About That Base by Meghan Trainor

Shake It Off by Taylor Swift

Baby Don't Lie by Gwen Stefani

This Is How We Do by Katie Perry

Gunshot by Lykke Lei

Under The Gun by Sisters of Mercy

Over It by Crystal Method

Stay Awake by Ellie Goulding

Blame by Calvin Harris

Walks Like Rhianna by The Wanted

Devil Within by Digital Daggers

Centuries by Fall Out Boy

Reach by Imagine Dragons

Lockdown by Amy Lee

Monsters by Sarah McLaughlin

Try by Colbie Calliet

Illusory Lights by Sara Blatsk

Heart 2015

Dear Future Husband by Megan Trainor

Heart by Mary Lambert

I Really Like You by Carlie Rae Jepson

Style by Taylor Swift

Rebel heart by Madonna

My Heartbeat Song by Kelly Clarkson

Young Blood by Bea Miller

London Queen by Charli XCX

Talking Body by TVO LO

All of Me by Betty Who

Ain't it Fun by Paramour

Leave Me by Imagine Dragons

I Live by OneRepublic

We Could Be Immortals by Fall Out Boy

Shut Up And Dance by Walk the Moon

Break Your Plans by The Fray

Thinking Out Loud by Ed Shereen

Stay With Me by Sam Smith

Love Is Just Another Way To Die

Eden 2015

Give It To Me by Allison Ireheta

Chandelier by Sia

Love Me Harder by Arianna Grande

Wildest Dreams by Taylor Swift

If You're Lips Are Movin' by Meghan Trainor

Living For Love by Madonna

Not Too Cool To Dance by Eden

Happy by 2NE1

Breaking Up by Charlie XCX

Burnin' Up by Jessie J

Big Booty by Jennifer Lopez

I'm Madonna Bitch by Madonna

We Can Be Heroes

Belagosi's Dead by CHVCH

Heart Wants What It Wants by Selena Gomez

Black Spacy by Taylor Swift

Secret by Mary Lambert

Down To The River

Adele Live

Spark 2015 Spring

Song 5 by Haim

Timber by Ke$ha

Something's Happening To Me by Arum Rae

One Hot Mess by Malea

Falling Down

Insomnia by Parson James

Ghostown by Madonna

Strangers by Seven Lions with Myon

Erasure by Sacred

Tear My Heart by 21 Pilots

Lampshade's on Fire by Modest Mouse

Renegade by The X Ambassadors

Dead Inside by Muse

What Kind Of Man by Florence and Machine

Biscuit by Ivy Levan

Need UR Love by Charlie XCX

Nobody Love by Tori Kelly

Title by Meghan Trainor

Yellow 2015 Summer

Perfect by 5 Seconds of Summer

Steal My Girl by One Direction

Safe and Sound by Capital Cities

Right by Echosmith

Yellow Flicker Beat By Lorde

Dark Paradise by Lana Del Rey

Two Weeks by FKA Twigg

Good For You by Selena Gomez

Cool For The Summer by Demi Lovato

Fight Song by Rachel Platton

Masterpiece by Jessie J

Firestones by Kygo and Conrad Sewell

Hold My Hand by Jessie Glynn

Neon Signs

No Sleep Janet Jackson

Ship to Wreck by Florence and the Machine

Fall Into The Sky by Zedd and Ellie Goulding

Feel The Light by Jennifer Lopez

Case For Shame by Moby

Today 2016

Hello by Adele

Invincible by Kelly Clarkson

Today's the Day by Pink

Use To Love You by Gwen Stefani

Wildest Dreams by Taylor Swift

Flesh without Blood by Grimes

Good Day for Love by Bonnie McKee

Confident by Demi Lovato

Love Hurts by Jojo

Gold by Kiera

Irresistible by Fallout Boy

Made of Stone by Evanescence

Dreams by Beck

I Promise by Captain Artic

Dibs by Kelsey

Till It Happens by Lady Gaga

Waiting by Sam Smith

Tomorrow 2016

When We Were Young by Adele

Steady by Rachel Platton

Hands To Myself by Selena Gomez

All of You by Betty Who

You Are My Summer by La+ch

Never Come Down by Brave New Stories

Monsters by Ruelle

On My Mind by Ellie Goulding

Redose by The Prototypes

Fog by Kids N Chemicals

Holy Dove by Civil Twilight

Bring Me Back To Life by HT Bristol

Here by Allyssa Cara

Indigo Puff by Layla

Elephant by Hannah George

Live Like Legends by Ruelle

Don't Come Over Jessie

Stand In Line by Baniff

Lazarus by Bowie

Little Man (70s) by Sonny and Cher

Unsteady 2016

Piece by Piece by Kelly Clarkson

No by Meghan Trainor

Try Everything by Shakira

Run on Love by TLOV

Locked Away by Rock City

Higher Place by Demetri

If On fire by V

Cake by the Ocean by DNCE

Crime on The Dance Floor by Thrust

The Moment by Tempe Impala

Cheap Thrills by Sia

Work by Rhianna

Pillow Talk by Zyan

Magnets by Lorde

Stolen Car by Sting and Myclen

California Dreamin'

Teas by Salt Cathedral

Until We Go Down by Ruelle

Unsteady by X Ambassadors

Ophelia by Lumineers

Keep Me A Secret by TVA

Truly Madly Deeply 2005 Love

I Could Fall In Love by Selena

All The Man That I Need by Whitney Houston

From This Moment On by Shania Twain

Spend A Lifetime Loving You by Marc Anthony

Spanish Guitars by Toni Braxton

Wonderful Tonight by Eric Clapton

Tonight and The Rest of My Life by Nina Gordon

I Wanna Love You Forever by Jessica Simpson

All I've Ever Wanted by Mariah Carey

My Heart Will Go On by Celine Dion

Runaway by The Corrs

Rush, Rush by Paula Abdul

The Woman in Me by Heart

Take My Breath Away by Berlin

Breathe by Faith Hill

I Love You by Sarah MacLauchlan

Love Hurts 2005 Break-Ups

Lover Hurts by Nazareth

Total Eclipse of the Heart by Bonnie Tyler

All At Once by Whitney Houston

December by Expose

How Can I Ease The Pain by Lisa Fischer

Ti Amo by Laura Braningan

Listen To Your Heart by DHT

It Must Have Been Love by Roxette

Tears in Heaven by Eric Clapton

Without You by Mariah Carey

Unbreak My Heart by Toni Braxton

The Color of the Night by Laura Christy

Insensitive by Jan Ardin

Foolish Games by Jewel

Torn by Natalie Imbruglia

Because of You by Kelly Clarkson

Hurt by Christina Aguilera

Night Club: Deseriah Destiny Soundtrack

My Funny Valentine Sung By Michelle Pfeiffer

The Way We Were by Barbara Streisand

The Rose by Bette Midler

Out Here On My Own by Irene Cara

Could Have Been So Beautiful by Tiffany

Foolish Beat by Debbie Gibson

Crazy for You by Madonna

Saving All My Love For You by Whitney Houston

Season's Change by Expose

Time After Time by Cyndi Lauper

Eternal Flame by The Bangles

I Get Weak by Belinda Carslile

I Still Believe by Brenda K

Love Don't Live Here Any More by Madonna

You Give Good Love by Whitney Houston

You Make Me Feel Like A Natural Woman

I Think It's Gonna Rain Today by Bette Midler

Unzipped Soundtrack 2007

Lady in Red by Chris DeBurgh

Saving All My Love For You by Whitney Houston

Self-Control by Laura Braningan

Throb by Janet Jackson

Angel by Jon Secada

Will You Still Love Me Tomorrow by Carole King

The Color of the Night by Laura Christy

Ti Amo by Laura Braningan

Love Don't Live Here Anymore by Madonna

Nobody Wants To Be Lonely by Ricky Martin

You Outta Know by Alanis Morrisette

I'm The Only One by Melissa Ethridge

Anything But Down by Sheryl Crow

Call Me When You're Sober by Evanescence

Cold by Crossfate

Saving Me by Nickleback

Wish You Were Here by Pink Floyd

More: Ben Mix

Dust In The Wind by Kansas

Hotel California by The Eagles

Do You Think of Me by Mariah Carey

That's The Way Love Goes by Janet Jackson

Runaway Train by Soul Asylum

Never Get Over You Getting Over Me by Expose

How Can I Ease the Pain by Lisa Fischer

To The Moon by Savage Garden

Fallin' by Alicia Keys

Rapture by Iio

Behind Blue Eyes by Limp Bizket

Broken by Seether and Amy Lee

More by Tara MacLean

My Immortal by Evanescence

Cup of Coffee: Ethan McMillan

Crush by Jennifer Paige

La Luna by Belinda Carlisle

Nothing Matters by Madonna

What Would Happen If by Meredith Brooks

Uninvited by Alanis Morrisette

Artificial Sweetener by No Doubt

Wild by Poe

Du Hast by Rammstien

Da Da Da by Trio

I & I by Tajia Seville

To The Moon by Savage Garden

Out of My Mind by Duran Duran

Cup of Coffee by Garbage

I Will Remember You by Sarah McLaughlin

Unconditional by Alanis Morrisette

Power of Goodbye by Madonna

Beyond The End: Mariah Carey Favorites

1990-2003

Love Takes Time

I Don't Want To Cry

And You Don't Remember

Can't Let Go

Until The End of Time

Do You Think of Me

Without You

Everything Fades Away

All I've Ever Wanted

When I Saw You

I Am Fee

Butterfly

My All

Whenever You Call

After Tonight

Bring on The Heartbreak

Jenny From The Block

1999-2003

If You Had My Love

Waiting For Tonight

Let's Get Loud

No Ame Ames

Un Noche Mas

Love Don't Cost A Thing

Play

Carino

Ain't It Funny

Jenny From The Block

I'm Glad

Baby I Love You

Firework: Katy Perry

2008-2013

Roar

Dark Horse

ET

Wide Awake

Firework

Part of Me

California Girls

Teenage Dream

Last Friday Night

I Kissed A Girl

Hot and Cold

Waking Up in Vegas

One of the Boys

Perfectly Pink

2000-2013

Try

True Love

Blow Me (One Last Kiss)

Perfect

Stupid Girls

Don't Leave

So What

Who Knew

God Is A DJ

U and UR Hand

Trouble

Get The Party Started

Family Portrait

Misery

Just Like A Pill

Most Girls

Complicated: Avril
2003-2013

Rock and Roll

Here's To Never Growing Up

Let It Go

Blackstar

Alice

Girlfriend

So Good

Pieces of My Heart

Keep Holding On

What I Wanted

Nobody's Home

Happy Ending

Fall To Pieces

I Don't Give A Damn

Sk8er Boi

Complicated

Jem and the Holograms

Theme

Truly Outrageous

She's Got The Power

Twilight in Paris

First Love

I Got My Eye On You

Deception

I'm Still Here

Can't Get My Love Together

Love Will Unite Us

Like A Dream

We Can Change It

We Can Make A Difference

Who Is He Kissing

Falling In Love With A Stranger

Friend or Stranger

Dear Diary

Land of the Midnight Sun

Shangri-La

You'll Never Win

Alone Together

Bet This

Glitter and Gold

I Believe In Happy Endings

Misfits

Young Blood (2015 Movie)

We've Got Heart (2015 Movie)

Zumba Class 2015

Cupid Shuffle by Cupid

Rain Over Me by Marc Anthony

Fireball by Pitbull

Zumba Ay Zumba Ah by DJ Mam

Coco No by Roberto Jr.

C'mon and Dance by Zumba

Indian Moonshine by Banghra

Waka Waka by Shakira

Mr Saxobeat by Alexandra Stan

Supergirls by Mara Prada

Livin La Vita Loca by Ricky Martin

Love Shack by The B52s

Latin Pop 1995-2015

Biddi Bidi Bom by Selena

I Could Fall In Love by Selena

Angel by Jon Secada

Just Another Day by Jon Secada

Lifetime Loving You by Marc Anthony

I Need To Know by Enrique Iglesias

Bailimos by Enrique Iglesias

Spanish Eyes by Ricky Martin

No Ame Ames by Jennifer Lopez

Waiting for Tonight by Jennifer Lopez

No One Wants To Be Lonely by Ricky Martin & Xtina

Genie in a Bottle by Christina Aguilera

Dance With Me by Debra Morgan

Wherever, Whenever by Shakira

Post Modern Juke Box 2013-2015

Thrift Shop

Fancy

Dark Horse

Wake Me Up

Chandelier

Take Me To Church

Cadillac

Just Dance

All About That Base

Timber

Creep

Barbie Girl

Sk8er Boi

Shake It Off

Just Dance 2

Young and Beautiful

Talk Dirty To Me

Careless Whisper

Digital Download/Burned

Compilation Albums

Adele (19/21)

Beatles (#1s)

Beethoven

Belinda Carlisle (Greatest Hits)

Bessie Smith (1923-1933)

Blacklist Soundtrack

Bryan Adams (Greatest Hits)

Care Bears On Fire

Candlebox 1994

Celtic Women (Believe)

Cher (Greatest Hits)

Chicks on Speed (99 Cents)

Collette (Push)

Crow Soundtrack

David Bowie (Greatest Hits)

Delirium (Best Of)

Diva Christmas

Dresden Dolls (Coin/No)

Drop Kick Murphy's (Signed, Sealed)

Eclectic: Dallas String Quartet 2010

Enya

Evelyn, Evelyn

Emile Autumn (Opheliac)

Girls Soundtrack (S1 and 2)

Imagine Dragons

Kerli (Love Is Dead)

Jem (Finally Awoken)

Lestat (Grave/Sorrows)

Lily Allen (2009)

Lily and Madeline 2013

Lily Hayden (1997)

Live (Awaken: Best of)

My So-Called Life Soundtrack

Nadia Ali

Night Wish

Nirvana (Never/Utero/Unplugged)

No Doubt (Greatest Hits)

Plumb (1997-2007)

Ramones Greatest Hits

Rock Star INXS

Sarah MacLauchlan (Illusion/Shine On)

Selena Gomez

Sheryl Crow (Greatest Hits)

Swedish House Mafia (Until Now)

Sons of Anarchy Soundtrack (S1-4)

Taylor Swift (Red/1989)

Xandria

Zedd (Clarity)

Artists in Media Player

2015

Artist	Songs	Albums
3 Doors Down	16	7
Weird Al	117	5
10,000 Maniacs	4	1
The 1975	2	1
Ace of Base	18	3
Adele	33	2
Aerosmith	74	10
Afro-Celts	1	1
The Afters	4	1
Aimee Man	3	1
Airborne Toxic Event	1	1
Alana Miles	1	1
Alicia Keys	6	2
Alison Krause	11	1
The All American Rejects	3	2
Alanis Morrisette	110	14
ATC	1	1
Atlas Genius	5	1
Attack, Attack	5	1
Avicii	3	1

Avril Lavigne	82	
AWOL Nation	14	1
Ayla	1	1
Aryia	4	2
Amber	12	2
Ally and AJ	14	1
Angelic	1	1
Anjulia	1	1
Angelfish	4	1
American Authors	1	1
Allison Ireah	13	1
Alt J	8	1
Apple Tree and Tangerines	1	1
Armin Van Buren	1	1
Ashley McIsaac	1	1
Atlantic Star	1	1
Audio Slave	1	1
Aurora	1	1
B52s	19	2
Bad English	2	1
Baha Men	1	1
The Bangles	6	1
Barbara Streisand	14	1
Basement Jaxx	1	1

Bastille	18	1
Bat For Lashes	13	1
The Beach Boys	40	1
Belle and Sebastian	2	1
Belly	18	1
Belinda Carlisle	23	3
Berlin	1	1
Bessie Smith	49	1
Bette Midler	3	1
Beyoncé	9	1
Bif Naked	13	1
Billie	1	1
Billie Myers	1	1
Billy		
Corrigan	12	1
Black Sabbath	14	1
Blondie	31	3
Birdy	11	1
Billy Thorpe	1	1
Black Veil Brides	12	1
Blur	6	1
Blu Cantrell	14	1
Blue Oyster Cult	6	1
Bodeans	1	1
Bonnie McKee	1	1

Bonnie Tyler	1	1
Boston	8	1
Bowling For Soup	54	2
Boyz II Men	2	1
Breaking Benjamin	13	1
BT	1	1
Brandy	2	2
Brian Seltzer Orchestra	2	1
Buckcherry	20	1
Buffalo Tom	3	1
Blue Man Group	14	1
Bon Jovi	29	3
Bush	7	1
Butthole Surfers	1	1
Buzcocks	14	1
The Beatles	55	1
Cake	29	3
Calvin Harris	18	1
Camper Van Beethoven	20	1
Candlebox	39	3
Carebears on Fire	12	1
Carly Simon	14	1
Carol King	35	10
Carrie Underwood	7	2

Cary Brothers	2	1
Cascade	2	1
Celine Dion	27	6
Chad Kroger	1	1
Celtic Women	15	1
Charlie		
XCX	1	1
Chemical Brothers	13	2
Cher	21	1
Cherie	12	1
Cheyanne Kimball	13	1
Cherry Poppin Daddies	14	1
Chicks on Speed	31	1
Chris De Burg	1	1
Christina Aguilera	13	5
Courtney Love	12	1
CCR	20	1
The Corrs	52	5
The Civil War	8	1
Colbie		
Callie	10	2
Collette	13	1
Cradle of Filth	12	1
The Cranberries	53	3
Crossfate	1	1
Crystal Method	21	2

Cyndi Lauper	4	4
DHT	3	1
Daft Punk	3	1
Dadga	10	1
The Damwells	13	1
Dar Williams	12	1
Darude	2	1
Daughtry	12	1
David Arkenstone	27	2
David Bowie	21	2
David Parsons	6	1
Dead Kennedys	21	1
Dead Milkmen	6	1
Dead Sara ·	13	1
Deadeye Dick	1	1
Dead Eanson	9	1
Deanne Johnson	1	1
Debbie Gibson	15	2
Deborah Harry	14	1
Debra Morgan	1	1
Deep Purple	22	2
Def Leopard	12	1
Deftones	2	2
Delirium	97	11
Delta Ray	1	1

Demi Lovato	18	2
Destiny's Child	8	2
Dianne Warren	1	1
Die Krupps	9	1
Dirty Vegas	6	1
Dixie		
Chicks	15	2
DJ Shadow	17	1
DJ DB	1	1
DJ Samy	1	1
DJ Tiesto	10	1
DJ Yaure	1	1
Donna Summer	3	1
The Donnas	38	3
The Doors	19	1
Dr. Jeffery Thompson	1	1
Dream	1	1
Dresden Dolls	42	3
Drop Kick Murphy's	28	2
Dum Dum Girls	10	1
Duke Spirit	12	1
Duran Duran	7	2
Eagle Eye Cherry	1	1
Eagles	13	3
Eels	1	1
Eiffel 65	1	1

Elastica	1	1
Elbow	1	1
Elisa Forillo	1	1
Ellie Goulding	36	3
Emile Sand	14	1
Enigma	62	6
Enya	19	2
Elton John	5	2
Emile Autumn	23	1
Epica	2	1
Eric Carmen	1	1
Estheo	17	1
Escape Fate	1	1
Euphoria	1	1
Eurhythmics	3	2
Evanescence	22	4
Evans Blue	1	1
Eve	1	1
Evelyn Evelyn	13	1
Expose	17	3
The Exies	1	1
Fame	2	1
Faith Hill	8	2
Faithless	13	1
Fat Boy Slim	17	2
Fastball	1	1

Fall Out		
Boy	5	1
Fiest	12	1
Fergie	2	1
Filter	2	1
Finger Eleven	13	1
Firewater	1	1
Flaming Lips	1	1
Fleetwood Mac	17	1
Flogging Molly	28	2
Florence and the Machine	12	1
Fluke	3	3
Fly Leaf	30	3
Foghat	1	1
Foreigner	3	3
Foster The People	1	1
Four Non-Blonds	1	1
Fragma	1	1
The Fray	15	2
Fuel	1	1
Fun	4	1
Fun Loving Criminals	1	1
Future Sounds of London	1	1
Gang Star 1998	7	1
Garbage	64	6
Gin Blossoms	27	2

Gina G	1	1
Girls Generation	1	1
Gloria Estefan	9	1
Goyte	1	1
Gravity Kills	3	1
God Lives Underwater	3	2
Godsmack	3	2
Golano	12	1
Good Charlotte	19	2
Great White	14	1
Greenday	50	6
Green Jelly	1	1
Gregorian Sarah	1	1
Grimes	2	2
Groove Armada	13	1
Guns N Roses	16	2
Gustavo Santalallo	1	1
Gwen Stefani	15	1
Hannah Montana	26	8
Hans Zimmer	1	1
Harvey Danger	1	1
Haley Wisteria	13	1
Heart	50	3
Hinder	7	1
Hole	8	2

Hooverphonic	15	2
Hum	1	1
Icona Pop	1	1
Iio	2	1
Ilsa Forillo	1	1
Imagine Dragons	30	3
Imani Coppela	1	1
Inhibited	11	1
Inxs	39	3
Iron and Wine	1	1
Itzhak Perlman	14	1
Ivana Van Dahl	2	1
Ivy	13	1
JS Bach	9	1
Jaykle	2	1
Jade	2	1
James Asher	11	1
Jan Arden	2	2
Jane Jensen	11	1
Janet Jackson	60	5
Janis Joplin	12	1
Jared Leto	1	1
Jefferson Starship	1	1
Jem	11	1
Jem and the Holograms	16	1
Jennifer Lopez	80	8

Jennifer Paige	1	1
Jessie J	7	2
Jessie Robinson	1	1
Jessica Simpson	10	2
Jessie Bayle	1	1
Jessie Ware	1	1
Jet	13	1
The Jets	1	1
Jewel	75	5
Jill Souble	1	1
Jim Brickman	1	1
Joanna	10	1
Johann Brahms	13	1
John Coltrane	9	1
John Verily Band	1	1
John Williams	1	1
Johnny Cash	31	1
Jojo	2	1
Jon Secada	5	1
Jonathan Peters	1	1
Jordan Sparks'	1	1
Jordis Unga	4	1
Joy Formidable	12	1
Juliana Hatfield	2	1
Juno Reactor	5	2
K's Choice	1	1

KT Tunstall	1	1
Kansas	1	1
Karmin	4	1
Kate Bush	1	1
Kate Vogel	9	1
Katherine McPhee	13	1
Katy Perry	40	3
Kelly Clarkson	70	7
Kelly Osborne	1	1
Kerli	12	1
Kim Wilde	1	1
Kimberly Locke	12	1
Kimya Dawson	4	1
Kinky	14	1
Kitaro	15	2
Kongos	1	1
Korn	1	1
Kraftwork	1	1
Kreo	1	1
Kristin Hersh	14	1
Kylie Minogue	14	3
La Bouche	3	1
La Tigre	1	1
Lacuna Coil	31	3
Lady Gaga	30	3
Ladyhawk	10	1

Lady Tron	2	2
Laibach	1	1
Lana Del Rey	2	1
Laura Braningan	2	1
Laura Christy	2	1
Lautspecher	1	1
The Lawyer	1	1
Led		
Zeppelin	13	3
Lemonheads	1	1
Lenka	2	1
Lenny Kravitz	3	3
Leanne Rimes	1	1
Leona Lewis	19	2
Lestat	12	2
Letters to Cleo	12	1
Life In		
Mono	1	1
Lights	7	1
Lili Hayden	10	1
Lilly Collins	1	1
Lily and Madeline	10	1
Lilly Allen	12	1
Limp Bizket	1	1
Linda Ronstadt	1	1
Lisa Fischer	5	1

Lisa Loeb	2	2
Lisa Marie Presley	7	1
Little Dragon	1	1
Live	58	6
Liz Phair	70	3
Lorde	11	1
Lorena McKennett	34	3
Lucas	1	1
Luce	1	1
Ludwig Von Beethoven	11	1
Lumineers	1	1
Luscious Jackson	5	2
Lykki Li	1	1
Lynard Skynard	3	1
M2M	1	1
M83	1	1
Madonna	100	7
Marc Brown	13	3
Mandy Moore	15	2
Manheim Steamroller	18	1
Marc Anthony	2	2
Marc Shiman	1	1
Marcy's Playground	3	1
Mariah Carey	100	18
Marianne Faithful	16	1
Maria Digby	12	1

Marilyn Manson	1	1
Maroon 5	12	1
Martika	2	1
Marty Casey	2	2
Match Box 20	4	2
Mazzy Star	1	1
MC Hammer	1	1
Meatloaf	11	1
The Medieval Babes	17	1
Meiko	1	1
Melissa Ethridge	20	3
Meredith Brooks	2	1
Michael Giacchino	21	1
Michelle Branch	3	2
Michelle Pfeiffer	1	1
Mig Ayses	1	1
Mighty, Mighty Bosstones	2	2
Mika	1	1
Miley Cyrus	2	2
Minnie Driver	11	1
Mister Mister	1	1
Moby	70	5
Moldy Peaches	1	1
Mona	1	1
Mya	2	2
Myudyvane	12	1

Moneen	1	1
My Chemical Romance	2	1
Mythos	13	1
Monica	2	1
MZM	1	1
Nadia Ali	4	3
Natacha Atlas	8	1
Natalie Imbrulia	3	2
Nazareth	1	1
Nelly Furtado	2	1
New Order	1	1
Nick Cave & The Bad Seeds	16	1
Nickleback	46	5
Nicole Cross	1	1
Nightwish	10	1
Nina Gordon	1	1
Nine Inch Nails	16	6
Nirvana	20	3
The Nixons	1	1
No Doubt	65	5
Nonono	1	1
Norah Jones	5	1
Nox Arcana	1	1
Oakenfold	2	2

Offspring	40	4
Oona	1	1
Orbital	11	1
Original Soundtrack	0	55
Oanette Coleman	1	1
Otherwise	3	1
Our Lady Peace	12	1
Pink	45	10
Paramour	3	1
Passenger	12	1
Pat Benatar	4	1
Patrick Swayze	1	1
Patty Smyth	25	2
Patti Smith	1	1
Paul Oakenfold	32	2
Paul Van Dyk	34	1
Paula Abdul	18	2
Paula Cole	30	3
Peaches	1	1
Pearl Jam	2	1
Persephone's Bees	11	1
Philip Philips	13	1
PJ Harvey	10	1
Pink Floyd	13	3
Player	1	1
Plumb	28	2

Poe	25	2
Poison	1	1
The Police	3	2
Portished	12	2
Presidents of USA	8	1
Primus	44	4
Prince	3	1
Prodigy	3	1
Puddle of Mud	4	1
Quad City Djs	1	1
Queen	29	2
Quarterflash	12	1
Queens of the Stone Age	8	1
REM	13	2
Ra Ra Root	2	1
Radiohead	12	1
Rainbow Brite	1	1
Rammstien	28	3
Ramones	25	6
Reba McIntire	1	1
The Refreshment	1	1
The Rembrandts	1	1
REO Speedwagon	1	1
Republica	7	1
Rhianna	1	1
Richard Marx	17	1

Ricky Martin	11	2
Right Said Fred	1	1
Rilo Kelly	26	2
Rob Thomas	2	2
Rob Zombie	32	2
Robin Fox	13	1
Rose Murphy	1	1
Roi Golen	1	1
Rosie Thomas	1	1
Roxette	2	2
Rui Da Silver	1	1
Run Lola Run	1	1
Rusted Root	39	2
Ryan Star	1	1
Sad Alice Said	1	1
Sade	1	1
Salt N Pepa	1	1
Samantha Mumba	1	1
Santana	16	1
Sara Barillas	15	3
Sarah Connor	1	1
Sarah Harmer	11	1
Sarah McLaughlin	72	4
Sarina Paris	1	1
Sausage	8	1

Savage Garden	12	2
Saving Jane	10	1
The Scorpions	1	1
Seal	2	2
Seether	25	2
Selena Gomez	14	4
Senses Fail	11	1
Sex Pistols	1	1
Shakespeare's Sister	3	1
Shakira	26	3
Shania Twain	34	3
She Wants Revenge	1	1
Sheryl Crow	46	4
Sia	1	1
Siouxe and the Banshees	10	1
Sir Mix A		
Lot	1	1
Six Pence Non The Richer	1	1
Skid Row	4	1
Skye Sweetninam	14	1
Sky Dance	13	1
Skillet	34	3
Sky Ferria	1	1
Skyler Grey	12	1
Smash Mouth	3	2
Sneaker Pimps	1	1

Soko	1	1
Son by Four	1	1
Sonia Dada	12	1
Sonic Youth	15	2
Sonique	1	1
Sophie B Hawkins	3	2
Soul Asylum	1	1
Soul Decision	1	1
Sound Garden	16	1
Stabbing Westward	3	2
The Starting Line	1	1
Starship	1	1
Stereo Lab	1	1
Steven Halpern	11	1
Stone Temple Pilots	17	1
Straylight Run	11	1
Styx	16	1
Sublime	3	1
Sugarland	11	1
Sunscream	13	1
Supernova	11	1
Supreme Beings of Leisure	1	1
Suie McNeal	1	1
Swedish House Mafia	23	1

Sweet Sensation	1	1
Switchblade Symphony	10	1
Switchfoot	12	1
System of a Down	11	1
Tatu	11	1
Trio	1	1
Tajia Seville	2	1
Talking Heads	8	1
Tripping Daisy	2	1
Tara McLean	22	2
Taylor Dane	2	1
Taylor Swift	2	1
Teagan and Sara	1	1
Telekinesis	1	1
Theory of a Deadman	14	2
Thalia	14	1
Thievery Corporation	7	1
They Might Be Giants	24	2
Tiffany	2	1
Tina Arena	1	1
Tityo	1	1
TLC	4	2
Toadies	1	1
Toby Lightman	1	1
Tom Petty	7	2
Toni Braxton	8	3

Tool	15	1
Tori Amos	70	5
Traci Spencer	1	1
Turin Breaks	1	1
TV on the Radio	1	1
TV Themes	10	1
U2	2	1
Underworld	3	3
Urge Overkill	1	1
Uriah Heap	9	1
Vampire Weekend	8	1
Vanessa Williams	2	2
Velvet Underground	1	1
Violent Femms	5	1
Verruca Salt	3	2
Vitamin C	1	1
VNV		
Nations	2	1
The Walkman	2	1
Walter Jackson	1	1
The Wanted	1	1
War	1	1
Wednesday	14	1
Weezer	7	2
Westworld	1	1
When Boy Meets Girl	1	1

White Lion	1	1
Whitney Houston	30	3
Wicked Wisdom	2	1
Will Smith	17	1
Willa Ford	11	1
William Orbit	2	1
Winger	1	1
The Wreckers	1	1
Xandria	13	1
Yani	33	3
Yo Yo Ma	1	1
Zamfir	18	1
Zedd	10	1
Zendaya	1	1
Zuny	10	1
ZZ Ward	13	1
	6817	930

www.ingramcontent.com/pod-product-compliance
Lightning Source LLC
Chambersburg PA
CBHW081351280526

45788CB00009B/2845